World Military and Social Expenditures 1982

Ruth Leger Sivard

"The care of human life and happiness, and not their destruction, is the first and only legitimate object of good government."

Thomas Jefferson, US, 1809

Acknowledgments

This edition attempts to focus attention on the effects of the world arms race, looking not only at the nuclear threat but also at the broad dangers to the economic welfare, to human rights, and to life itself. In preparing the material, I owe a debt to many who have given both encouragement and professional support.

Norman Waitzman, whose assistance has been indispensable throughout the project, has conducted an interesting study of militarization and repression. Paul Walker has once more contributed his expertise to the presentation on nuclear weapons, which has also benefitted from William Arkin's extensive research on nuclear deployment. William Eckhardt prepared the historical record on wars and the casualties associated with them.

Laura Cover, Isabelle Osborne, Pierre Fabre (France), and Paul Ticher (UK) made important contributions to various aspects of the background research.

I am also indebted to Gordon Ewing and to Alfred McAdams, who have generously volunteered aid and professional advice in times of need.

Marjorie Ewing continues to give support on numerous administrative matters. Jim Sivard, who has tried valiantly to help with circulation while keeping up with his profession in music, has had to resign in the face of a rising tide of orders. Laura Cover will be in charge of circulation beginning with this edition.

It should be emphasized that interpretations of the factual material are my responsibility and do not necessarily reflect the views of the sponsoring organizations.

Washington, D.C., August 1982

FOREWORD

Viewed from space, the Earth seems exquisite and serene, carried by its star on a journey that by now is 4.5 billion years long. When we look more closely we find that life and intelligence have arisen and evolved on this world, and have filled it with a profusion of beauty. The most advanced species has in only a few centuries worked technological wonders, and is entirely able to provide for each of its 4.4 billion members. But when we look more closely still, we find that the vast majority of the individuals of this species lead lives of misery and despair, never tasting the intellectual, bodily, and spiritual fulfillment of which they are capable. Soon they will be spending a trillion dollars a year on past, present, and future military activities. They have stockpiled an arsenal of over 17,000 targeted strategic weapons that can destroy their global technology and perhaps their species. They exhibit extreme devotion to various national, ethnic, religious and economic doctrines, but hardly ever wonder about the wellbeing of the planet.

What would an extraterrestrial observer, with no emotional stake in the outcome of terrestrial events, make of all this? In provincial isolation, we see only small pieces of the picture. But if we step back, if we embrace a planetary perspective, the picture that emerges is so clear, its implications so dangerous, that any thoughtful person must be moved to action. The annual surveys of world military and social expenditures, written by Ruth Leger Sivard, are an indispensable introduction to that planetary perspective.

Carl Sagan

CONTENTS

The purpose of this report is to provide an annual accounting of the use of world resources for social and for military purposes, and an objective basis for assessing relative priorities. In bringing together military costs and social needs for direct comparison, the report bridges a gap in the information otherwise available to the public. It is hoped that this will help to focus attention on the competition for resources between two kinds of priorities. Future issues will attempt to improve the coverage with additional measures, monetary and non-monetary, of the state of the world.

Summary

History's most expensive arms race is also proving to be the most costly in terms of world security. The overhanging threat is nuclear catastrophe on a scale to end life on earth.

The extremes of militarism in 1982 are manifest in other ways that endanger the public safety. There have been hostilities on five continents. Major military states stretch tentacles of power and tension into distant areas of the world. Lightning advances in technology make the weapons of today more dangerous to civilians than to the armed forces involved. In developing countries, political processes are increasingly under military control, and civil rights are widely violated. Even in industrialized democracies, decisions on military matters appear unresponsive to the public will.

For the global economy, military expenditures of $600 billion a year have become the 20th century's burden of Sisyphus. Relative to the economy, the burden is growing larger. While business in the military sector is booming, recession grips world markets, stifling economic advance, driving up unemployment, adding new millions to the numbers of the impoverished, the uneducated, the underfed.

1982 has been a poor year for security of both people and nations. On the other hand, it may stand as a harbinger of change. Still to be fully tested is the effect on world priorities of a growing multitude of people determined to speak out against military mania.

Priorities 1982

The world's stockpile of nuclear weapons is equivalent to 16,000 million tons of TNT. In World War II, 3 million tons of munitions were expended, and 40-50 million people died.

The US government is spending a minimum of $4,500 million a year on a rapid deployment force to protect its vital interests in Middle East oil, vs $400 million for research on renewable energy sources as alternatives to oil.

In 24 countries, food consumption averages 30 to 50 percent above requirements; in 25 countries the average is 10 to 30 percent below requirements.

The richest fifth of the world's population has 71 percent of the world's product; the poorest fifth has 2 percent.

The international policing effort to control the proliferation of nuclear weapons has an annual budget of $30 million, half the size of the average police budget of a medium-large US city.

In 32 countries, governments spend more for military purposes than for education and health care combined.

Nuclear missiles can go from western Europe to Moscow in 6 minutes, but the average rural housewife in Africa must still walk several hours a day for the family's water supply.

The NATO and Warsaw Pact forces between them have 100,000 tanks. Tailgating each other, they would form a column stretching from Paris to Budapest.

The efficiency of a US car (fuel use to weight) has doubled since World War II; the efficiency of a nuclear weapon (destructive yield to weight) has increased 150 times.

In the US, the world's first superpower, one person in seven lives below the poverty threshold.

In the USSR, the world's second superpower, the infant mortality rate is over twice the average for other developed countries.

The family breadwinner in industrial countries works one and one-half weeks per year to pay for national military forces; 4 minutes a year to pay for international peacekeeping.

Military Expansion

In the highly charged world of 1982, military expansionism appears to be the dominant dynamic force. The continued upward thrust of all basic indicators of military power is in striking contrast to the global economic decline and, the evidence indicates, bears a heavy responsibility for it.

Chart 1 portrays four of the measurable features of the arms race of the 1980s. These are:

☐ Astronomical costs, now reaching above $600 billion a year, or well over one million dollars a minute.

☐ Twenty-five million people serving in the regular armed forces, backed 3 to 1 by reserves, paramilitary forces, and the civilians needed to produce the weapons and services essential for their operation.

☐ An international trade in conventional arms, now over $35 billion a year, proliferating sophisticated weapons of war into the most remote and least developed areas of the world.

☐ An uncontrolled buildup of nuclear weapons, at present equal to an explosive force of 3.5 tons of TNT for every person on earth.

Illustrating the military expansion of the period since 1960, the trend lines of chart 1 also throw light on the future. If growth continues at the same rate, by the year 2000 national governments will have spent an additional $15 trillion (in today's prices) on military defense. Furthermore, by 2000 at least 8 million more men will be added to the regular armed forces; the value of arms traded will approach $100 billion a year; and the number of strategic nuclear warheads threatening human existence will be more than double the overkill of today.

After the expenditure of so much more of its treasure on military defense, will the world be a safer place in the year 2000 than it is today? Reasonable people will differ in their answer to that question, but in looking ahead it may be useful to review, from a global perspective, what security the arms race has bought in the years since 1960.

No world war, no nuclear holocaust has occurred. *But*

. . . In "local" wars, at least 10 million people have died, more civilians than soldiers.

. . . The aggressive sale of sophisticated weapons throughout the developing world has raised tensions and the violence of local conflicts; by arming potential enemies, it also threatens the security of the exporting nations as well.

. . . Technological advances blur the distinction between weapons of mass destruction and conventional arms; there has been a quantum jump in the kill-power of weapons.

. . . With an enormous and growing nuclear stockpile, power has become centralized to an unprecedented degree; the decisions of a few men now hold all of humanity hostage.

. . . As military power has grown, civil rights have weakened, including the public right to safety under the law and citizen control of the processes of government.

. . . Under its heavy military burden, the global economy has also suffered. The diversion of resources from civilian needs is a silent killer, curbing productivity and development, and adding more millions to the hundreds of millions of people lacking the most basic necessities of life.

In summary, the $9 trillion spent for "defense" in the last decades appears to have diminished rather than strengthened world security. The chapters following will look more closely at these and other effects. First we might consider why, despite the sorry record of the past, the military momentum appears to be undiminished. At the risk of oversimplification, four factors are identified in the pages immediately following. The nuclear buildup is treated separately.

State of the World's Military Machine

The trend is toward expansion, whether measured in government budgets, men under arms, research effort, number of weapons or their kill-power.

Further growth will be on top of new records in all indicators of military development. In financial terms, this means current annual outlays of:

$600,000,000,000 in military expenditures
50,000,000,000 in weapons research
35,000,000,000 in arms trade

And a record weapons inventory, including
150,000 tanks
40,000 combat aircraft
50,000 nuclear weapons

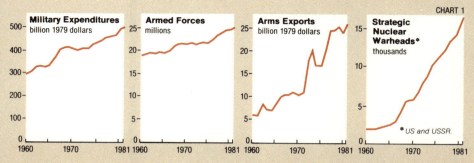

Military Expenditures
billion 1979 dollars

Armed Forces
millions

Arms Exports
billion 1979 dollars

Strategic Nuclear Warheads*
thousands

* US and USSR.

CHART 1

"We are in danger of arming ourselves into oblivion".
Admiral Hyman G. Rickover
United States, 1982

Size

An unusual power structure has been created by the arms race of recent decades. It is a relatively new phenomenon. In earlier years war departments tended to shrink between major wars, and equipping military forces was a comparatively small industrial enterprise. Today an estimated 100 million people world-wide are engaged directly or indirectly in military activities—a population larger than that of any country in the world except the big five: US, Brazil, USSR, India, and China.

The military bureaucracy is unique not only in size but in the financial resources and political influence at its command. Within most central governments, military employees represent a major share of the public payroll and administer the largest slice of the government budget, on average accounting for one-fifth of the public revenue.

In the arms-producing countries, military procurement has created multinational industrial giants and one of the most prosperous and powerful industries in the world. Aided by aggressive government promotion in foreign markets, the arms business now enjoys an estimated $150 billion in annual sales, ranking in size just below the annual incomes of the world's fourteen largest national economies.

The military presence exerts a growing influence on political life. It supplies the trappings of power for political leaders—jet aircraft, honor guards, a budget that can easily absorb hidden luxuries. It also affects the conduct of the public business. Secrecy becomes more important. The nation's security is increasingly identified with military security. One threat, the threat of armed attack, becomes the dominant concern, and the requirements of deterrence provide a rational, built-in growth factor.

Superpowers

Two nations representing 11 percent of the world population have spearheaded and shaped the global military competition since World War II. The US and USSR lead in the development and refinement of new forms of warfare. They spend half the world's military budget[1], export 58 percent of the arms moving in international trade, and control 96 percent of the world's stockpile of nuclear weapons.

Only two economic giants could have mobilized the resources required for the extraordinary competition in which they have been engaged. Both countries, the USSR especially, have used a larger-than-average share of an expanding economic base to support the military effort. Super budgets and an unchallenged technological lead ensure that the two powers can continue to dominate the pace and direction of the arms race into the future.

Advanced technology has also brought the whole world within the

1. See pages 38-39 for a discussion of the uncertainties in estimates of Soviet military expenditures.

MAP 1

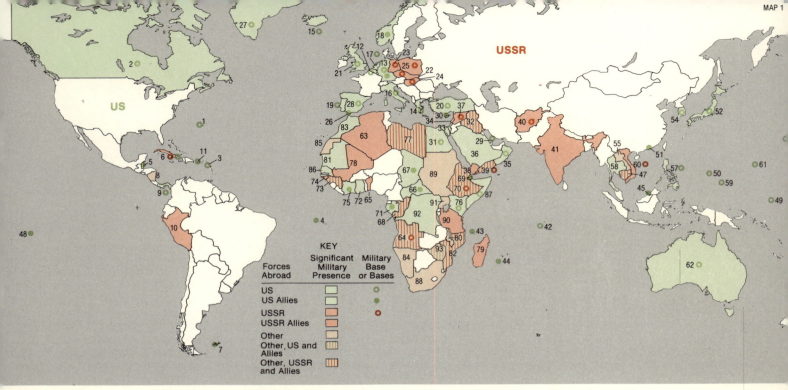

USSR

US

KEY

Forces Abroad	Significant Military Presence	Military Base or Bases
US		
US Allies		
USSR		
USSR Allies		
Other		
Other, US and Allies		
Other, USSR and Allies		

Military Bases and Personnel on Foreign Territory*

Bases and forces abroad project military power far from home territory. An incomplete record shows 93 countries and territories in which there is a foreign military presence, and at least 1,800,000 personnel involved. About one-quarter of the forces are at present fighting wars on foreign ground. The rest are abroad for a variety of reasons including: to support governments in power; provide training; conduct nuclear tests; establish a listening post or bases for ships or planes—a "defense" perimeter as far distant as the other side of the globe.

In the past year the US and USSR defense ministries had a non-lethal exchange of fire, in the form of propaganda leaflets. In each brochure was a map illustrating the adversary's threatening presence throughout the world. The map above attempts to fill out the picture, covering not only both superpowers but also their allies and others having bases and/or forces abroad, by invitation or invasion. Incomplete though information is so far, it portrays a world caught in a vast web of military entanglements. "Defense" has taken on global reach, at infinite risk to world security.

Countries of Origin

Locations of Foreign Forces	US and Allies**		USSR and Allies**		Other	
North America						
1 Bermuda	US	1,540	—		—	
2 Canada	US	710	—		—	
Latin America						
3 Antigua	US	120	—		—	
4 Ascension Is.	US	2,200	—		—	
	UK	na				
5 Belize	UK	na	—		—	
6 Cuba	US	2,250	USSR	12,000	—	
7 Falkland Is.	UK	na	—		—	
8 Nicaragua	—		—		C	3,200
9 Panama	US	9,150	—		—	
10 Peru	—		USSR	175	—	
11 Puerto Rico	US	2,940	—		—	
NATO Europe						
12 Belgium	US	2,380	—		—	
13 Germany, West	US	256,740	—		—	
	F,N,UK	138,000				
14 Greece	US	3,520	—		—	
15 Iceland	US	3,130	—		—	
16 Italy	US	12,760	—		—	
17 Netherlands	US	2,090	—		—	
18 Norway	US	210	—		—	
	UK	na				
19 Portugal	US	1,660	—		—	
20 Turkey	US	5,170	—		—	
21 United Kingdom	US	26,720	—		—	
Warsaw Pact						
22 Czechoslovakia	—		USSR	78,000	—	
23 Germany, East	—		USSR	406,000	—	
24 Hungary	—		USSR	50,000	—	
25 Poland	—		USSR	50,000	—	
Other Europe						
26 Gibraltar	UK	na	—		—	
27 Greenland	US	320	—		—	
28 Spain	US	7,700	—		—	

Locations of Foreign Forces	US and Allies**		USSR and Allies**		Other	
Middle East						
29 Bahrain	US††	—	—		—	
30 Cyprus	UK	na	—		—	
	Tu	20,000				
31 Egypt	US	180	—		—	
32 Iraq	—		USSR	8,000	C	2,200
			EG	180	Ir	50,000
33 Israel	US	110	—		—	
34 Lebanon	—		—		S	60,000
					I	90,000
35 Oman	US††	—	—		—	
36 Saudi Arabia	US	520	—		—	
37 Syria	—		USSR	4,000	—	
			EG	210		
38 Yemen, AR	—		USSR	475	—	
39 Yemen, PDR	—		USSR	2,500	C	800
			EG	325		
South Asia						
40 Afghanistan	—		USSR	87,000	C	100
41 India	—		USSR	1,550	—	
42 Diego Garcia	US	1,840	—		—	
43 Mayotte	F	na	—		—	
44 Reunion	F	na	—		—	
Far East						
45 Brunei	UK	na	—		—	
46 Canton Is.	US	†	—		—	
47 Cambodia	—		USSR	300	V	150,000
48 F. Polynesia	F	na	—		—	
49 Gilbert Is.	US	†	—		—	
50 Guam	US	8,680	—		—	
51 Hong Kong	UK	7,000	—		—	
52 Japan	US	50,450	—		—	
53 Johnston Atoll	US	120	—		—	
54 Korea, S.	US	37,560	—		—	
55 Laos	—		—		V	40,000
56 Midway Is.	US	†	—		—	
57 Philippines	US	14,050	—		—	
58 Thailand	US	100	—		—	
59 Trust Territory	US	†	—		—	
60 Vietnam	←		USSR	4,000	—	
61 Wake Is.	US	†	—		—	
Oceania						
62 Australia	US	700	—		—	

Locations of Foreign Forces	US and Allies**		USSR and Allies**		Other	
Africa						
63 Algeria	—		USSR	8,500	C	170
			EG	250		
64 Angola	—		USSR	700	C	8,000
			EG	450		
65 Benin	—		USSR	1,200	—	
66 Cen. Afr. Rep.	F	950	—		—	
67 Chad	F	na	—		—	
68 Congo	—		USSR	850	C	950
69 Djibouti	F	3,800	—		—	
70 Ethiopia	—		USSR	2,400	C	5,900
			EG	550		
71 Gabon	F	500	—		—	
72 Ghana	UK	150	—		—	
73 Guinea	—		USSR	375	C	280
			EG	125		
74 Guinea-Bissau	—		USSR	600	—	
75 Ivory Coast	F	450	—		—	
76 Kenya	US††	—	—		—	
	UK	100				
77 Libya	—		USSR	2,300	C	3,000
			EG	1,600		
78 Mali	—		USSR	636	—	
79 Madagascar	—		USSR	370	—	
80 Malawi	·		—		SA	100
81 Mauritania	F	110	—		—	
82 Mozambique	—		USSR	500	C	1,000
			EG	100		
83 Morocco	F	150	—		—	
84 Namibia	—		—		SA	50,000
85 Sahara, W	—		—		M	21,000
86 Senegal	F	600	—		—	
87 Somalia	US††	—	—		—	
88 South Africa	—		—		I	200
89 Sudan	—		—		E	700
90 Tanzania	—		USSR	300	—	
91 Uganda	—		—		T	1,000
92 Zaire	F	100	—		—	
	B	350				
93 Zimbabwe	UK	380	—		Ch	120
					NK	200

TOTAL PERSONNEL	B Belgium 350	E Egypt 700	M Morocco 21,000	S Syria 60,000	UK United Kingdom .. 76,530
	Ch China 120	F France 57,860	N Netherlands 5,500	T Tanzania 1,000	USSR 722,731
	C Cuba 25,600	Ir Iran 50,000	NK N. Korea 200	Tu Turkey 20,000	V Vietnam 190,000
	EG E. Germany 3,790	I 90,000	SA S. Africa 50,000	US 455,620	

*Unless a base is indicated, the list covers only those locations where reported foreign personnel number 100 or more. Soviet and Soviet allied personnel, as estimated by the US DOD, include **civilian** advisors; others do not. "Foreign territory" includes overseas areas associated with or administered by US, UK, and France.*

**NATO and Warsaw Pact (members of alliances, page 27.)
†less than 100 personnel
††facilities under construction

For sources and qualifications of the data, see page 36.

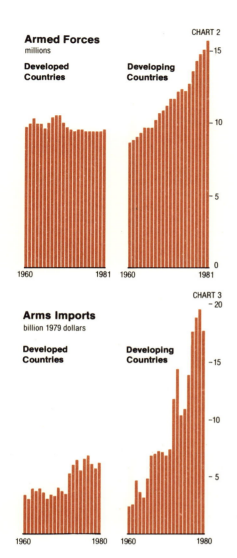

Armed Forces
millions

Developed Countries   **Developing Countries**

CHART 2

1960   1981   1960   1981

Arms Imports
billion 1979 dollars

CHART 3

Developed Countries   **Developing Countries**

1960   1980   1960   1980

Unrecorded Channels of Arms Proliferation

Official transfers of conventional arms amount to an estimated $35 billion a year. This total may be only a drop in the bucket of proliferation, since it does not cover trade outside regular official channels, nor the many routes, direct and indirect, through which the technology of weapons production spreads internationally. The black market in arms alone is said to be a multi-billion dollar industry.
Some of the unrecorded channels of international proliferation are:

    Licensed production
    Co-production
    Industrial espionage
    Military advisors
    Training of foreign forces
    Thefts from overseas arsenals
    Official but covert arms supply
    Covert military operations
    Black market trade

orbit of this bipolar competition. As *map 1* illustrates, each of the superpowers has established a network of forward bases and listening posts worldwide. An estimated two-thirds of military personnel deployed on foreign territory are theirs. Through a chain of alliances, they have encouraged polarization around their own East-West views of world security.

In summer 1982 there are no hopeful signs of an early thaw in the Cold War. The bellicose rivalry between the two countries has deep roots in mutual fear, reinforced over the years by each side's exaggerated views of the strength and designs of the opponent. Fear and rhetoric have de-humanized the enemy. Suspicion has become an addiction, generously fed by the self-interests of powerful bureaucracies.

Proliferation

Twenty years ago developing countries accounted for only 10 percent of world military expenditures; their share has since doubled. As *chart 2* shows, it is in the poorer countries that all of the rise in armed forces has occurred since 1960; their forces now represent two-thirds of the world's total. Arms imports of developing countries have risen even more sharply *(chart 3)*; in 1980, they amounted to $20 billion, three-fourths of world arms trade.

Local and regional arms races are not a new phenomenon. What is new in today's militarism is the nature of the weaponry that is proliferating and the war-fighting technical skills which have been developed. Encouraged by the uninhibited export drive of the major powers, even the poorest countries now have access to the most advanced forms of military technology

Trade is only one of many channels of diffusion, as the list below suggests. Virtually every developing country has had armed forces trained by the major powers, communist or western, and quite a few have had help from both sides. In 1981 alone the US provided military training to forces from 60 developing countries, the UK to trainees from 23 developing countries. Where arms go, advisors and technicians follow. In the next stage of military development there is a demand for local arms production. Over 30 countries in the Third World are now producing weapons, some as complex as fighter aircraft and missiles. For developing countries, sophisticated weapons, professional soldiers, and a fledgling arms industry have come to represent the symbols of nationhood. They also foster a political leadership and entrenched bureaucracy oriented to power through further military expansion.

Weapons research

Research to produce more complex, accurate, and lethal instruments of war dominates the world's publicly-supported research effort. In the past year the governments of nine western European countries and the US spent $29 billion on military research, as well as $6 billion on space research which has major military applications. Rough estimates suggest that a global total of about $50 billion is spent annually on military research and development, and that nearly one-half million scientists and engineers are employed in the effort.

Aided by the enormous resources which military programs command, science in recent years has radically altered the nature of warfare. Many of the most revolutionary modifications have occurred in the so-called conventional arms, which take the largest share of military budgets even in nuclear weapons states. Technological advances have moved the potential battlefield into everyone's backyard. Targets can be destroyed from great distances. Explosive power has been vastly enhanced. Weapons are precision-guided and more accurate, and at the same time capable of massive and indiscriminate destruction.

Huge annual investments in military research have paid off in a technological advance that is unmatched in the civilian field. They also contribute another powerful, self-generating feature to the arms race. The competition can no longer be described simply as an action-reaction phenomenon between potential enemies. What the technology can produce, the weapons inventory wants.

The Nuclear Race

No aspect of the arms race more sharply defines a competition out of control than the huge and continuing buildup of nuclear weapons. Since their development and first use in warfare, these weapons have increased at a phenomenal rate. About 50,000 nuclear bombs and warheads are now in existence, scattered worldwide. The explosive force that they represent is more than one million times the power of the single bomb that leveled Hiroshima. The growth in number of weapons and in their destructive capacity is only part, however, of the escalating nuclear danger.

It is true that 37 years after the atomic devastation of Hiroshima and Nagasaki only five states (US, UK, USSR, France, and China) are officially recognized to have nuclear weapons in their arsenals, and 118 states have agreed, under the Non Proliferation Treaty (NPT) of 1968, not to manufacture or otherwise acquire nuclear weapons or other nuclear explosive devices. Despite these signs of restraint, the nuclear situation is highly volatile, representing a threat to civilization that mounts daily.

Two forces combine to drive the nuclear race, Atoms for Peace and Atoms for War work in tandem, spreading dangerous tinder over the face of the earth. *Map 2* following shows the reactors and weapons sites, the research, production, storage, and waste sites of The Nuclear World of 1982.

Nuclear power — The commercial use of nuclear energy for electric power had a later start than the development of nuclear weapons. The first power reactor came on line in 1954, twelve years after the first research reactors had produced fuel for nuclear weapons. Since then the industry's growth has been rapid *(chart 4)*. There are now 279 operating power reactors and at least 323 research reactors in 54 countries.

Several factors have aided the nuclear industry's expansion: the effort by rich and poor countries to explore and exploit this new technology, especially as an energy source for electric power; active marketing of the extremely expensive equipment and fuel needed for nuclear operations; and, not least, government support and subsidization. Official interest in nuclear energy has in fact been a critical element in its development. Governments have fostered research, aided in the training of specialists, subsidized trade, and insured even the privately-owned industry against potentially disastrous losses.

Through the growth of the peaceful atom, nuclear technology and expertise have spread widely. Bomb-grade material has as well. As a by-product of its operations, the average commercial reactor yields about 500 pounds of plutonium a year. Plutonium in waste fuel can be separated chemically and used to manufacture nuclear weapons. Counting all power reactors now in operation, the potential from this source alone is about 7,000 bombs a year.

Peaceful facilities therefore provide a direct and potentially clandestine route to the proliferation of weapons. But this is not the only connection between peaceful and military uses of nuclear energy, nor the only aspect endangering security. Throughout the production process there are interconnectons and associated dangers—dangers of theft, terrorism, release of radioactivity, sudden catastrophe. And at the end of the process there is a legacy for future generations in the unsolved problem of disposing of the deadly nuclear waste generated by both peaceful and military uses.

Nuclear weapons—The first nuclear weapons demonstrated a power of destruction so awesome as to bring an abrupt halt to war in Japan. The gravity bomb used on Hiroshima had an explosive power equivalent to about 15,000 tons of TNT. It weighed five tons, and required a heavy bomber to transport it. The single bomb leveled a city of 350,000, killing one person in four immediately. Twice as many died in the next 5 years.

In destructive power, accuracy, means of delivery, as well as numbers, there has been a revolutionary change in nuclear weapons since those

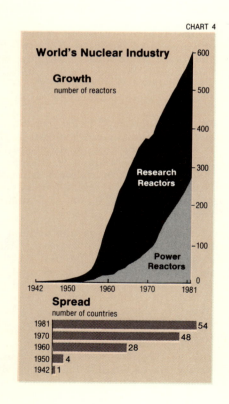

CHART 4

World's Nuclear Industry

Growth
number of reactors

Research Reactors

Power Reactors

1942 1950 1960 1970 1981

Spread
number of countries

1981 — 54
1970 — 48
1960 — 28
1950 — 4
1942 — 1

CHART 5

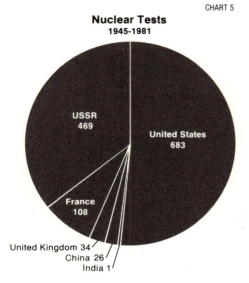

Nuclear Tests
1945-1981

USSR
469

United States
683

France
108

United Kingdom 34
China 26
India 1

CHART 6

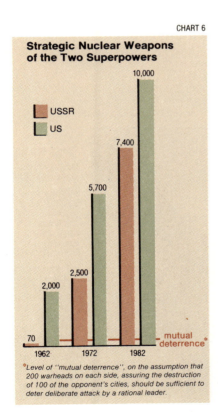

Strategic Nuclear Weapons of the Two Superpowers

USSR
US

10,000
7,400
5,700
2,500
2,000
70

mutual deterrence*

1962   1972   1982

*Level of "mutual deterrence", on the assumption that 200 warheads on each side, assuring the destruction of 100 of the opponent's cities, should be sufficient to deter deliberate attack by a rational leader.

first "primitive" bombs. There has been an equally radical development of official concepts about their use. The fundamental changes that have occurred in both technology and strategy are necessary for an understanding of the terrifying implications of the nuclear arms race today.

Since 1945 over 1,300 nuclear test explosions have occurred *(chart 5)*. The rate of testing has gone up in recent years. In 1981, it averaged about one explosion per week. A dedicated research effort, with repeated testing, has produced very major changes in the ability of nuclear weapons to hit and destroy targets. Each weapon can now deliver considerably more punch (yield) relative to its weight. The improved yield-to-weight ratio means that a strategic warhead today, e.g., on the US Poseidon submarine, has increased in efficiency 150 times as compared with the Hiroshima bomb.

Increased efficiency means that mini nukes are now possible. Nuclear weapons can be made small enough for battlefield use—or to carry in a suitcase. It also means incredibly rapid flight time to the target. The larger, strategic variety can travel from one continent to another (6-8,000 miles) in less than 30 minutes. Intermediate-range missiles can make the distance from western Europe to Moscow or vice versa in 6 minutes; the bomber of the 1950s would have taken 3 hours for the same trip.

Now a single delivery vehicle (missile, bomber, submarine) can also deliver more bombs to a target, or hit more targets, more precisely. The Poseidon submarine (US) carries 16 missiles, each with 10 warheads, each warhead with an explosive force over three times that of the Hiroshima bomb. Conceivably a single submarine could destroy 160 targets, more targets than there are cities in the USSR. It can deliver over twice as much explosive force as all the munitions of World War II, in which 40-50 million people were killed. One submarine represents only a small fraction of the nuclear power available to each of the superpowers.

Technology and the weapons that it has created have clearly surpassed the concept of nuclear force as the means of deterring war *(chart 6)*. True, the minimum amount of threatened destruction considered necessary for deterrence was never officially spelled out. How much of his country in ruins, how many of his countrymen instantly killed, would stop a rational leader from initiating nuclear war? Three nuclear weapons powers, France, UK, and China, apparently consider less than 200 strategic weapons a sufficient deterrent. The US, however, has 10,000, the USSR 7,400, and both are building more.

Under the deterrent concept, each side recognized its vulnerability in event of nuclear war. Any use of nuclear weapons would inevitably escalate, and destruction would be mutual. Since there is no defense against the weapons, and also no possibility of eliminating the opponent's ability to retaliate, destruction was also assured. Mutual assured destruction (MAD) was a vision of horror, but as the rationale for nuclear forces it was better than what we seem to have now.

With radical advances in accuracy and power, deterrence has been subject to challenge on two grounds. One is that land-based nuclear weapons are vulnerable to destruction if the enemy strikes first, thus eliminating the power of retaliation. The other is that the use of nuclear weapons in a graduated, carefully-orchestrated manner can be an integral part of war-fighting strategy. Both theories are dangerous fantasies. The first, because it assumes the perfection of a technology which has had a poor record for reliability. The second, because it assumes an absence of human error and a perfection of discipline (including under war conditions) which are unknown in reality.[2]

Nevertheless, the jump from a deterrent against war to usable *weapons of war* is now a feature of nuclear strategy, used to justify further escalation in numbers and technology. It also greatly magnifies the risk that these weapons will be used, and that nuclear war to extinction will result.

---

2. *For some examples of mechanical and human failure, see page 44; also page 15 in* World Military and Social Expenditures 1981.

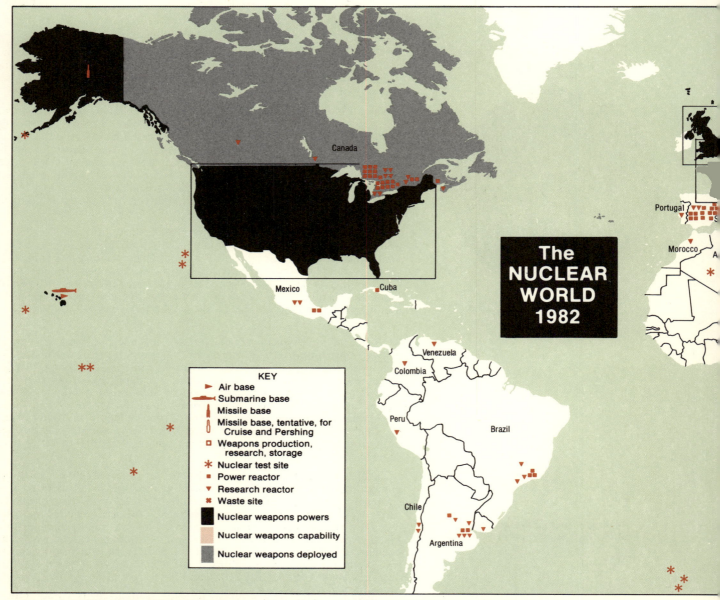

The NUCLEAR WORLD 1982

KEY

- ► Air base
- ◄►— Submarine base
- ▮ Missile base
- ▯ Missile base, tentative, for Cruise and Pershing
- ☐ Weapons production, research, storage
- ✳ Nuclear test site
- ■ Power reactor
- ▼ Research reactor
- ✕ Waste site
- ⬛ Nuclear weapons powers
- ⬜ Nuclear weapons capability
- ⬛ Nuclear weapons deployed

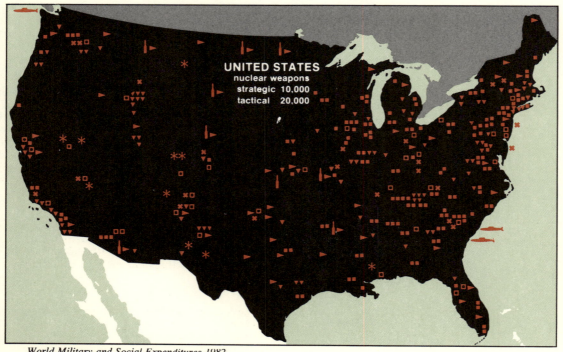

UNITED STATES
nuclear weapons
strategic 10,000
tactical 20,000

The Nuclear Network

now reaches across six continents and three oceans

Military uses are represented b[y]
50,000 weapons of mass des[-]
truction, ready for delivery fro[m]
an armada of submarines, su[r-]
face ships, aircraft, and fro[m]
missiles and artillery with range[s]
from 10 to 8,000 miles.

Five countries are officiall[y]
known to possess nuclea[r]
weapons. They have bases [or]
ports of call in at least 20 foreig[n]
countries and territories. The[ir]
weapons have been tested [at]
sites as distant as Africa an[d]
Pacific islands.

Commercial uses are represen[-]
ted by 602 power and researc[h]
reactors in 55 countries. Onc[e]
promoted as Atoms for Peac[e,]
these uses also carry dangers [of]
mass destruction, through ma[l-]
function, sabotage, radiatio[n,]
deadly nuclear wastes, and th[e]
diversion of their byproduct, plu[-]
tonium to weapons production.

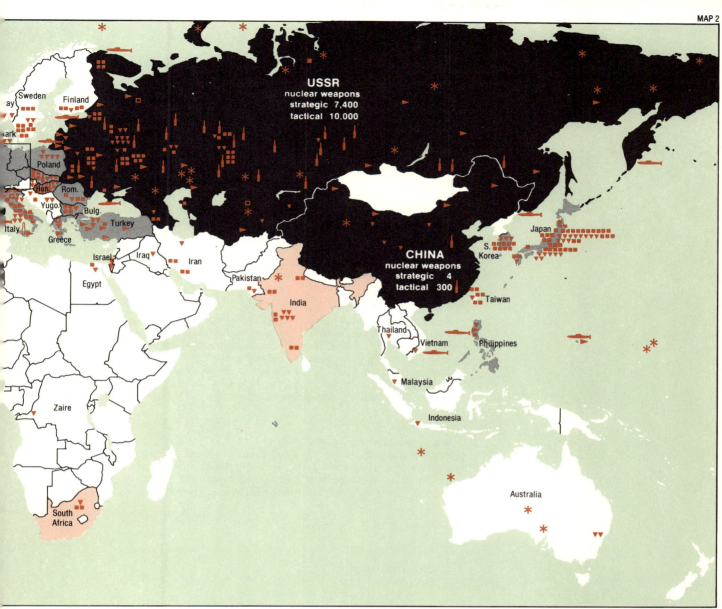

MAP 2

Sweden
Finland

ay

ark

Poland

Hun. Rom.

Yugo.

Bulg.

Turkey

Italy

Greece

USSR
nuclear weapons
strategic 7,400
tactical 10,000

Israel   Iraq   Iran

Egypt

Pakistan

India

CHINA
nuclear weapons
strategic   4
tactical   300

S.
Korea

Japan

Taiwan

Thailand

Vietnam   Philippines

Malaysia

Zaire

Indonesia

Australia

South
Africa

**UNITED
KINGDOM**
nuclear weapons
strategic 192
tactical 250

Netherlands

Belgium

Switz.

FRANCE
nuclear weapons
strategic   80
tactical   300

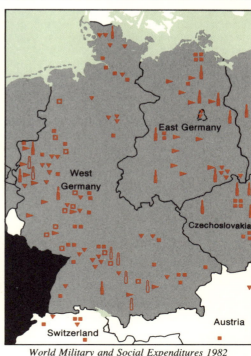

East Germany

West
Germany

Czechoslovakia

Austria

Switzerland

Boomerang

Far from making the world a safer place, the race to arm for "defense" has undermined security. A nuclear Frankenstein is the most terrifying of its creations. No known menace equals it in its potential for the annihilation of humanity. The increase in the number and destructiveness of nuclear weapons, their reckless proliferation throughout the world, the spread among more nations of the capability to produce these weapons, the apparent lack of will by national governments to achieve control, combine to put all life in jeopardy (see pp. 41-44)

Beyond the nuclear menace, there seems to be no end to man's inhumanity to man, including himself. An uncontrolled arms race boomerangs from many directions. Rather than serving as the defense it is said to be, it recoils back and imperils the safety of the people it is intended to protect. In these pages, three of these dangers are illustrated: the rising toll of civilian life in modern war, the aggressive proliferation of arms which return to threaten the exporting nations, and the violation of human rights associated with military control over governments.

At a time of grave economic-social distress world-wide, there is nothing that is more needed for the health of all nations than an environment conducive to broad cooperative action. Instead, the atmosphere is dominated by bellicose rhetoric, an emphasis on military rather than social threats to security, and on military solutions to problems that in fact are deeply rooted in social conditions. The result is a rising level of tension in the world, accompanied by civil disorder and wars of increasing destructiveness.

Hostilities

No nation can stand aloof from this turmoil. All suffer, some indirectly, through economic and political debilitation. Others are engulfed directly in violent conflict. How many and how destructive of life wars have been in recent years are illustrated opposite *(map 3)*. Fought with weapons called "conventional", they have been responsible for well over 10 million deaths since

---

Boomerang!
Bullets Bite Back

Arms exports and the training of foreign forces are increasingly in favor with governments as a means of political influence and a source of foreign exchange. Unfortunately, national friendships are not always durable, nor can the final destination and use of arms be foreseen. For the citizen of the supplying countries and their military forces, the proliferation of weapons very often boomerangs. Their own arms are turned against them or are used in ways inimical to their security.

United Kingdom, one of Argentina's major suppliers, sent that country military equipment up to eight days before Argentina invaded the Falkland Islands in April 1982, and the two countries were at war.

France, ally of the UK, had supplied Argentina with the Exocet sea-skimming missile which demolished the British destroyer Sheffield. The missile included British-made components.

South Korea, a top recipient of US arms, manufactures American-designed equipment and sells to Libya, which the US refuses to supply.

United States, supplier of $7.4 billion in military aid to Israel between 1978 and 1981, found itself unable to halt the use of these weapons, including cluster bombs, in an Israeli blitzkrieg into Lebanon in 1982.

Libya received 20 tons of US-made plastic explosives through an illicit shipment arranged by a former American CIA agent.

Nicaragua's Sandinistas overthrew the regime of dictator Somoza (which the US had supported), with arms largely purchased on the black market in Miami, USA.

Israel, which supplied arms clandestinely to Iran during the Iraq invasion of Iran, subsequently faced Iranian volunteers in its war in Lebanon.

China, a major supplier of arms to North Vietnam until 1978, went to war against it in 1979 and faced some of its own weapons in a short but bloody war.

USSR fought rebels in Afghanistan who were armed with weapons it had previously provided to Egypt, or which Egypt had manufactured from Soviet models.

And more merry-go-round—

In Vietnam, USSR now makes use of the large naval and air bases constructed by the US during the Vietnam war.

In Somalia, US is settling into the large Berbera base on the Indian Ocean, constructed by the USSR before it parted company with Somalia in 1977.

MAP 3

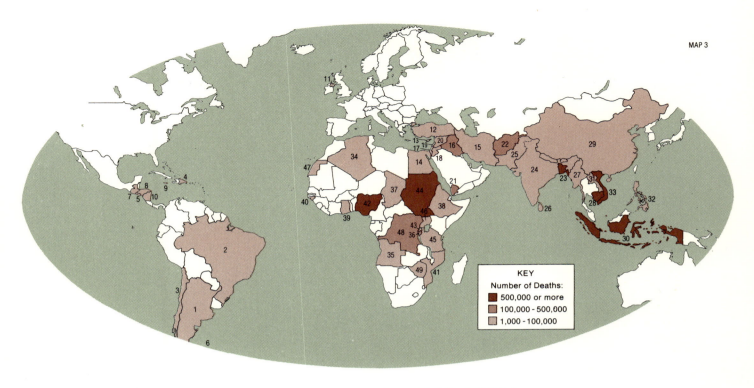

Wars and Deaths 1960-1982*

A new flare-up of hostilities in 1982 brings to 65 the number of major wars (deaths over 1,000) since 1960. They have been fought on the territory of 49 countries, representing approximately two-thirds of the world's population and 40 percent of its land area.

Recent wars have been grossly destrucitve of human life; that we know. More precisely, how many people have died and how many have been disabled as a result of this organized violence we will never know. On a subject which must be of considerable importance to all humanity, official records are notoriously silent. In every country the budget requirements for defense are laid out annually. Even the budgetary cost of war, in terms of the equipment destroyed that must be replaced, is totted up. The cost of war in terms of lives that can never be replaced seems to be of less interest to official agencies.

The statistics on war fatalities that are available are maintained largely by private organizations and concerned scholars. They are incomplete, particularly on the matter of civilian deaths. The total of 10,700,000 deaths shown in the table below is a partial accounting of the human cost which never appears in the world's official military expenditures.

Location	Years	Intervention[1]	Invasion[2]	Civilian	Battle	Total
Latin America						
1 Argentina	1975-79			na	na	7.000
2 Brazil	1980			na	na	1.000
3 Chile	1973			na	na	10.000
4 Dominican Rep.	1965	US		na	3.000	(3.000)
5 El Salvador	1976-			25.000	20.000	45.000
6 Falkland Is.	1982	UK	Argentina	na	1.000	1.000
7 Guatemala	1967			24.000	1.000	25.000
8 Honduras	1969		El Salvador	na	2.000	(2.000)
9 Jamaica	1980			na	na	1.000
10 Nicaragua	1977-79			15.000	35.000	50.000
Europe						
11 N. Ireland	1969-	UK		na	na	2.000
12 Turkey	1977-			na	na	5.000
Middle East						
13 Cyprus	1963-67	UN 64-		na	na	na
13 Cyprus	1973-79	Greece 74-75	Turkey 74-	3.000	2.000	5.000
14 Egypt	1967-70	Arab League	Israel	59.000	16.000	75.000
15 Iran	1978-		Iraq 80-82	na	na	14.000
16 Iraq	1961-75	Iran 61-67, 70-74		na	na	105.000
16 Iraq	1982		Iran	na	na	20.000
17 Israel	1973	Arab League	Egypt	na	17.000	(17.000)
18 Jordan	1970	Syria		na	2.000	(2.000)
19 Lebanon	1972-	Syria 76-, UN 78-		29.000	51.000	80.000
19 Lebanon	1982		Israel	9.000	1.000	10.000
20 Syria	1982			20.000	na	(20.000)
21 Yemen, AR	1962-69	Egypt 62-69		5.000	10.000	15.000
South Asia						
22 Afghanistan	1979-	USSR		90.000	10.000	100.000
23 Bangladesh	1971	India		1.200.000	300.000	1.500.000
24 India	1962		China	1.000	1.000	2.000
25 Pakistan	1965. 71	China 65	India	13.000	18.000	31.000
26 Sri Lanka	1971			na	2.000	(2.000)

Location	Years	Intervention[1]	Invasion[2]	Civilian	Battle	Total
Far East						
27 Burma	1980			na	na	5.000
28 Cambodia	1969-73	US 69-73	NVN 70-73	150.000	156.000	306.000
28 Cambodia	1975-78			2.000.000	na	(2.000.000)
28 Cambodia	1978-		VN 78-	na	50.000	(50.000)
29 China	1965-69			na	50.000	500.000
30 Indonesia	1965-66	China 65		na	na	500.000
30 Indonesia	1975-77			290.000	10.000	300.000
31 Laos	1960-73	US 61-73	NVN 65-73	50.000	24.000	74.000
32 Philippines	1972-80			30.000	30.000	60.000
33 South Vietnam	1960-75	US 61-73	NVN 65-75	500.000	1.500.000	2.000.000
33 North Vietnam	1964-73		US 64-67, 70-73	50.000	na	(50.000)
33 Vietnam	1979		China	9.000	21.000	30.000
Africa						
34 Algeria	1960-63	France 60-62		28.000	1.000	29.000
35 Angola	1961-	Portugal 61-75 Cuba 76-78	S. Africa 76-	48.000	7.000	55.000
36 Burundi	1972-73			50.000	50.000	100.000
37 Chad	1968-81	France 68-70. 78-79 Libya 71-81		na	na	3.000
38 Ethiopia-Ogaden	1961-	Cuba 77-78	Somalia 61-	10.000	15.000	25.000
38 Ethiopia-Eritrea	1962-	Cuba 78		na	30.000	(30.000)
39 Ghana	1981			na	na	1.000
40 Guinea-Bissau	1962-74	Portugal		na	na	15.000
41 Mozambique	1964-75	Portugal		na	na	30.000
42 Nigeria	1967-70. 81			1.000.000	1.000.000	2.000.000
43 Rwanda	1960-65			62.000	3.000	65.000
44 Sudan	1960-72			450.000	250.000	700.000
45 Tanzania	1978-79	Libya	Uganda	na	17.000	(17.000)
46 Uganda	1966			na	2.000	(2.000)
47 West Sahara	1975-		Morocco Mauritania 75-79	na	na	1.000
48 Zaire	1960-66	Belgium 60 UN 60-64. UK 64 Sudan 65		10.000	100.000	110.000
48 Zaire	1978	France		na	na	na
49 Zimbabwe	1965-79	Zambia 77		13.000	12.000	25.000

* *Wars* with recorded deaths of 1,000 or more.
1. *Intervention* by foreign forces or by the UN signifies overt action. and invitation by a recognized government. It is usually identified with a civil war.
2. *Invasion* is a hostile intrusion by a foreign country and includes air and missile attacks whether or not accompanied by land invasion. An intervening or invading country is identified in this table only when it was the first to take such action, and when the action was overt.
3. A bracketed figure indicates that an estimate has been obtainable only for battle deaths or only for civilian deaths. The total is therefore incomplete.

For sources and qualifications of the data, see page 36.

Repressive Regimes in the Third World
number of countries

CHART 7

Repressive Regimes in the Third World
number of countries

52	61
3	28
19	
30	23
	10
Military-Dominated Governments	Other Governments

■ Highly repressive, including torture and brutality.

▓ Repressive

□ None, or limited evidence

Official Arms Trade, 1976-1980, to Countries with Highly-Repressive Governments

million dollars

Supplying Countries	Value of Arms Deliveries to Countries with Highly-Repressive Governments	
	Military-Dominated	Other
USSR	$18,660	$ 3,880
US	5,275	6,800
France	2,910	1,740
Italy	1,685	520
W. Germany	1,330	520
UK	995	460
Czechoslovakia	865	70
China	340	10
Poland	270	30
Canada	85	15
Others	5,115	1,195
Total	37,530	15,240

Governments with the poorest records in human rights are big customers for foreign arms. During the five years ending 1980, they received two-thirds of all arms shipped to the Third World.

In total value of shipments, USSR was by far the largest supplier, with particularly heavy exports to Iraq, Syria, and Libya. The shipments of western suppliers were lower in total value, but more widely spread, reaching virtually all the highly repressive regimes.

1960. In this period there were 65 major wars (each causing at least 1,000 deaths). Over one-third of all nations in the world were caught up in physical violence, almost all of them in the Third World.

In 1982 alone, new and old wars have taken lives on five continents: in North America (El Salvador); South America (Falkland Islands); Europe (Northern Ireland); Asia (Afghanistan, Iran-Iraq, Lebanon); and Africa (Angola, Ethiopia-Somalia, Western Sahara). Most of the wars of 1982 are international, involving an invasion of one nation against another. In this respect they differ from the pattern of the last two decades, in which most wars were civil wars. Civil wars accounted for three-fourths of all deaths tabulated under map 2.

The historical record shows that to an increasing degree civilians are the main casualties of wars, whether they are international or civil. In the 1960s civilian and military deaths were about equal, but in the last decade civilian deaths rose sharply. The average in the later period is three civilian deaths to one battle death. A major reason for this is the increasingly sophisticated weaponry available even in developing countries, where most of the fighting has been. Weapons, fired from great distances, are more destructive and indiscriminate. Aided by mechanized equipment, conflicts fan out more rapidly, destroying crops and food supplies, causing floods of helpless refugees. Starvation takes many of them.

Since the wholesale bombing of World War II, wanton violence has become a common feature of modern war. It is no longer the men who fight but rather those for whom they are presumably fighting who become the main victims of war.

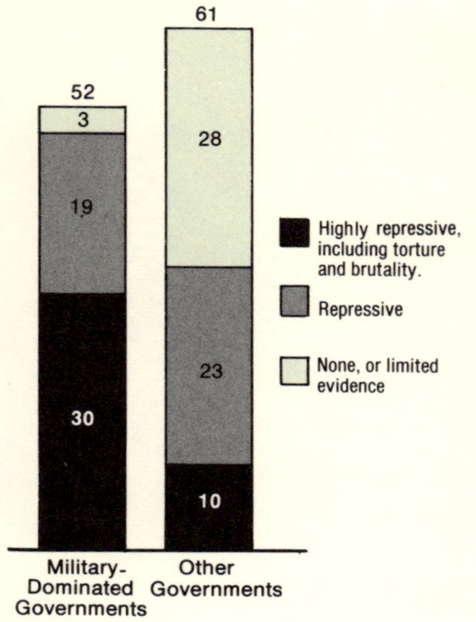

Repression

Militarism is a fascination with the use of force. It breeds war and makes it more destructive. It also increases internal political stresses and in itself becomes a major source of social turmoil. Extremes of repression are its hallmark.

The intrusion of military authority and influence into the political realm has been one of the fastest growing enterprises of the second half of this century. The armed forces have increased in numbers but the financial resources put at their disposal have expanded even more. Power grows out of the barrel of the gun and also out of the size of the budget.

In developing countries, where military expenditures (in constant prices) have increased twice as fast as the rapid rise in manpower, the military now have a dominant position in 46 percent of the governments (map 4). In every region of the developing world—Latin America, Asia, and Africa—they exert dominant control over approximately half of the national governments.

For the citizens, military control over the political processes means in many cases government less responsive to the needs of the majority of the population than to the requirements of those who have economic power. It means less political and press freedom, less opportunity for a gradual, evolutionary broadening of the development process to include all economic groups. In bottling up change, military-dominated governments also foster rebellion. They control it by the use of force against the populace. Repressive measures include arbitrary arrest, degrading treatment, brutality, torture, and summary execution.

Of the 52 governments identified as military-dominated, 49 in this year's survey were cited for violation of the citizen's right to safety under law (chart 7). Thirty practiced the most extreme forms of repression, including torture and brutality. Among other governments in the Third World, human rights records of many are far from good, but the incidence of the extreme forms of repression is much higher in the military-dominated (58 percent) than in the other governments (16 percent). In the ultimate mockery of "defense", military power wedded to political control turns inward to terrorize the people it is intended to protect.

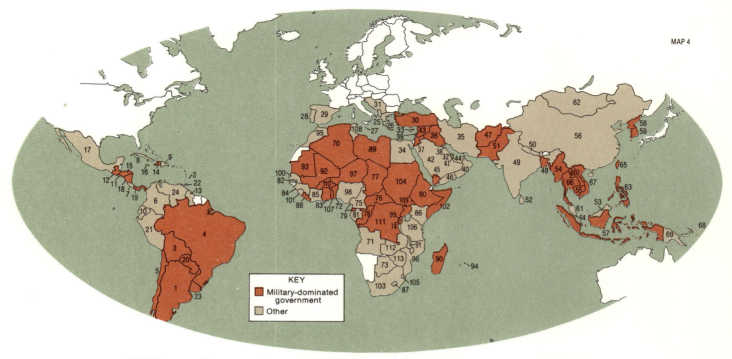

MAP 4

Military Control and Repression in the Third World*

Approximately half of all national governments in developing countries are now under military domination. This in itself is a startling situation, and perhaps even more so when one considers that the armed forces represent less than one-half of 1 percent of the population of Third World countries.

Not all will agree with the classification of all of these 52 countries as military-dominated. The criteria used, however, are fairly clear-cut and can be used to evaluate conditions in a particular country. One or more of the following characteristics was considered to be an indication of military control: a state of marshal law exists; military officers hold key positions in the political leadership; the regime was recently established by a military coup; the legal system is based on military courts; the military forces and political police are linked.

Among the governments characterized here as military-dominated, the human rights record is on the whole much more unfavorable than in other developing countries. On the basis of evidence reported by human rights organizations (see page 36), it appears that 49 of these 52 governments are repressive of the citizen's right to safety under the law, almost two-thirds of them showing a consistent pattern of extreme repression, including the use of torture (*chart 6,* opposite).

Military-Dominated Governments

Country	Coups 1960-82	Degree of Repression	Country	Coups 1960-82	Degree of Repression
Latin America			**Far East**		
1. Argentina	4	███	54. Burma	1	▒▒▒
3. Bolivia	8	███	55. Cambodia	1	▒▒▒
4. Brazil	1	███	57. Indonesia	1	███
5. Chile	1	███	58. Korea, N.	1	▒▒▒
11. El Salvador	2	███	59. Korea, S.	2	▒▒▒
12. Guatemala	2	███	60. Laos	—	███
14. Haiti	—	███	63. Philippines	—	███
15. Honduras	4	▒▒▒	65. Taiwan	—	███
18. Nicaragua	1	▒▒▒	66. Thailand	3	▒▒▒
19. Panama	2	▒▒▒	67. Vietnam	4	███
20. Paraguay	—	███			
23. Uruguay	1	███	**Africa**		
			70. Algeria	1	▒▒▒
Europe			72. Benin	4	▒▒▒
30. Turkey	2	███	74. Burundi	2	▒▒▒
			76. Central Afr. Rep.	3	▒▒▒
Middle East			77. Chad	1	▒▒▒
36. Iraq	1	███	78. Congo	1	▒▒▒
37. Jordan	—	▒▒▒	79. Equatorial Guinea	1	███
43. Syria	3	███	80. Ethiopia	2	███
45. Yemen, A.R.	3	▒▒▒	83. Ghana	5	▒▒▒
			88. Liberia	1	▒▒▒
South Asia			89. Libya	1	▒▒▒
47. Afghanistan	3	███	90. Madagascar	1	███
48. Bangladesh	4	███	92. Mali	1	▒▒▒
51. Pakistan	1	███	93. Mauritania	1	▒▒▒
			97. Niger	1	▒▒▒
			99. Rwanda	1	▒▒▒
			102. Somalia	1	▒▒▒
			104. Sudan	1	▒▒▒
			107. Togo	1	▒▒▒
			109. Uganda	3	███
			110. Upper Volta	3	▒▒▒
			111. Zaire	1	███

KEY

███ Highly Repressive, including torture and brutality

▒▒▒ Repressive

░░░ None, or limited evidence

Other Governments

Country	Coups 1960-82	Degree of Repression	Country	Coups 1960-82	Degree of Repression
Latin America			**Far East**		
2. Barbados	—	░░░	53. Brunei	—	░░░
6. Colombia	—	███	56. China	—	▒▒▒
7. Costa Rica	—	░░░	61. Malaysia	—	▒▒▒
8. Cuba	—	▒▒▒	62. Mongolia	—	░░░
9. Dominican Republic	1	▒▒▒	64. Singapore	—	▒▒▒
10. Ecuador	3	░░░			
13. Guyana	—	▒▒▒	**Oceania**		
16. Jamaica	—	▒▒▒	68. Fiji	—	░░░
17. Mexico	—	███	69. Papua New Guinea	—	░░░
21. Peru	4	███			
22. Trinidad & Tobago	—	░░░	**Africa**		
24. Venezuela	—	░░░	71. Angola	—	▒▒▒
			73. Botswana	—	░░░
Europe			75. Cameroon	—	▒▒▒
25. Albania	—	███	81. Gabon	—	▒▒▒
26. Greece	2	░░░	82. Gambia	—	░░░
27. Malta	—	░░░	84. Guinea	—	███
28. Portugal	—	░░░	85. Ivory Coast	—	▒▒▒
29. Spain	—	░░░	86. Kenya	—	▒▒▒
31. Yugoslavia	—	▒▒▒	87. Lesotho	—	▒▒▒
			91. Malawi	—	███
Middle East			94. Mauritius	—	░░░
32. Bahrain	—	▒▒▒	95. Morocco	—	███
33. Cyprus	1	░░░	96. Mozambique	—	▒▒▒
34. Egypt	—	▒▒▒	98. Nigeria	3	░░░
35. Iran	1	███	100. Senegal	—	░░░
38. Kuwait	—	▒▒▒	101. Sierra Leone	2	▒▒▒
39. Lebanon	—	▒▒▒	103. South Africa	—	███
40. Oman	1	▒▒▒	105. Swaziland	—	░░░
41. Qatar	1	▒▒▒	106. Tanzania	—	▒▒▒
42. Saudi Arabia	—	▒▒▒	108. Tunisia	—	▒▒▒
44. United Arab Emirates	—	░░░	112. Zambia	—	▒▒▒
46. Yemen, P.D.R.	1	▒▒▒	113. Zimbabwe	—	░░░

*The map and table identify only the 113 developing countries covered in WMSE 82.

For sources and qualifications of the data, see page 36.

South Asia		
49. India	—	███
50. Nepal	—	░░░
52. Sri Lanka	—	▒▒▒

Economic—Social Decline

The consequences of an unchecked arms race extend far beyond the direct links previously discussed: the growing threat of nuclear catastrophe, the rising death toll in hostilities, and the militarization of political authority. Another victim is the world economy. And in its immediate and long-term effects on human existence, this victim—barring nuclear war—may count as the most disastrous boomerang of all.

The military-economic connection must be seen in both developmental and welfare terms. In quiet, devious ways the military burden undermines the growth that is essential to sustain an increasing population. It slows civilian investment and productivity, stimulates inflation, widens the gap between rich and poor, and postpones the solution of overriding global problems which can be resolved only by all nations working in concert.

For those hundreds of millions of people living at the margin of existence, the military buden on society means unrelieved poverty and massive suffering. It condemns countless individuals to live out lives without hope, destitute of the most elementary needs. Like nuclear war, this too is genocidal.

In selecting for review four major features of today's troubled social condition, the summary following will also attempt to show their military connections. Because the economic effects of the arms race occur in hidden and roundabout ways, they are too often ignored in economic analysis. The purpose here is to bring them into better focus, not to deny the complex of influences of which they are one part.

Inflation

Stubborn price inflation is one of the most visible signs of a global economy in crisis. It is a pervasive, debilitating illness but uneven in its effects, bearing most heavily on the weakest members of society.

For over three years the world average of consumer prices has increased at an annual rate of 12-15 percent. No national economies, even those over which there is strong centralized control, can be sealed off from a virulent global inflation. All suffer, although not in equal degree. The poorest countries are the hardest hit. According to the IMF price index, inflation in the non-oil developing countries is currently more than twice as rapid as in the industrialized countries.

Within nations, the effects are also uneven. Again it is the poorest and weakest elements of the population, and particularly the elderly with fixed incomes, who bear a disproportionate share of the inflation burden. They have no margin of income to spare above minimum requirements for food and shelter. For them runaway inflation can mean the sacrifice of needs basic to life itself.

Military spending is a silent partner in the inflationary spiral, stimulating it in several ways. It generates spendable income without enlarging the supply of goods available in the civilian market. It draws off capital from civilian investment, which in turn slows productivity gains and price economies. The result is a generalized upward pressure on prices.

Military procurement also has a more specific inflationary impact which derives from characteristics peculiar to it: rapid product change and obsolescence, cost-plus-profit contracts, and the excessive waste endemic to large bureaucracies beyond public control. To ensure first claim on scarce materials, labor, management and scientific talent, military buyers operate under less price constraint than civilian buyers. Few economies can prevent this privileged demand from having a spill-over effect in the rest of the market.

Unemployment

The world economy is not able to provide jobs for its expanding work force. Rising unemployment has been a persistent problem, reflecting not only the sluggish growth of the most recent years but a longer-term serious weakness in the development process.

State of the World's People

While the military burden rises, the economic-social trend is toward further contraction, reflected in a slackening of economic activity and growing social distress.

The continued deterioration of the world economy follows several years of declining growth rates and accelerated inflation.

In human terms it means an increasing number of wasted lives:

  600,000,000 people unemployed or less than fully employed
  900,000,000 illiterate adults
  500,000,000 people malnourished
1,000,000,000 living in poverty

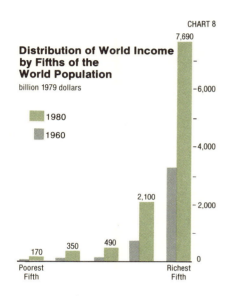

Distribution of World Income by Fifths of the World Population

billion 1979 dollars

CHART 8

■ 1980
■ 1960

7,690

2,100

490

350

170

Poorest Fifth

Richest Fifth

6,000

4,000

2,000

0

A sample of 50 countries for which records are available since 1960 suggests that the number of unemployed may be three to four times higher than it was 20 years ago. Precisely how many at any one time are out of work we do not know. Rough estimates indicate that there are at least 600 million people who are unemployed, or under-employed in the sense of not having enough work to rise above the poverty level. These 600 million represent close to 10 percent of the labor force in the western industrialized countries but up to 50 percent in developing countries. The rate of youth unemployment is substantially higher than the average.

Numbers alone cannot convey the scope of the problem, or the human tragedy it represents. For society as a whole it is an immense waste of potentially productive resources. Joblessness shows also in the frustration and alienation of a generation of young people, in rising crime rates, and in social unrest. It is a serious and growing threat to security of all nations.

Employment opportunities are linked to the availability of capital and the expansion of investment, a sustained growth in manufacturing, agriculture, and the service industries, and the training facilities needed especially for new entrants in the work force.

In all of these respects military expenditures are counterproductive. They have a negative impact on investment in civilian sectors; they divert research efforts to objectives that are not growth-producing; they train in skills largely unusable in the civilian economy. Studies in the US have shown that military expenditures create only half as many jobs as the equivalent amount of money spent on such basic needs of society as housing, roads, hospitals, schools. As an increasing number of developing countries have also found, defense spending is the least effective way to produce the job opportunities needed for rapidly growing populations.

Income inequality

The economic growth of recent years has failed to narrow the enormous gap between the richest and poorest countries and between rich and poor within countries. A few developing countries have successfully moved out of poverty into a dynamic pattern of growth based in part on rapid industrialization. Some of the oil-producing states have soared to record levels of per capita income. The average gain in income in developing countries, however, has been too small in absolute terms, the growth of population too great, to begin to shrink the income gap.

Chart 8 shows how the growth of GNP between 1960 and 1980 was distributed among income groups of the population. Calculated in constant prices, the annual per capita income of the poorest fifth of the population advanced about $54; for the richest fifth, the gain averaged $4,224. The gap between the top and low income levels more than doubled in absolute terms over the period.

In the developing world in particular, income extremes within countries also appear to have spread. It is not uncommon for the richest fifth in the country to command 60 percent or more of the national income, while the poorest fifth of the population shares 2 to 5 percent of it.

The increased military presence in the Third World countries contributes to continued inequalities within countries. Military-dominated governments resist change and tend to maintain feudal structures. With the land-owning and business classes, they establish first claim on economic gains. As a consequence, the dividends of growth are slow to trickle down to landless peasants and the urban poor.

The arms race also reenforces North-South inequalities. The impact of the rise in military expenditures has been relatively more severe in developing countries than in developed because of their much lower income base. Although the military burden relative to income has diminished somewhat in the last few years (and increased in the developed countries), the contrast between developed and developing in the income equivalents of their expenditures is still sharp. At 1980 levels of per capita income, military outlays represented 143 million man-years of imcome in developing countries and 50 million in developed.

MAP 5

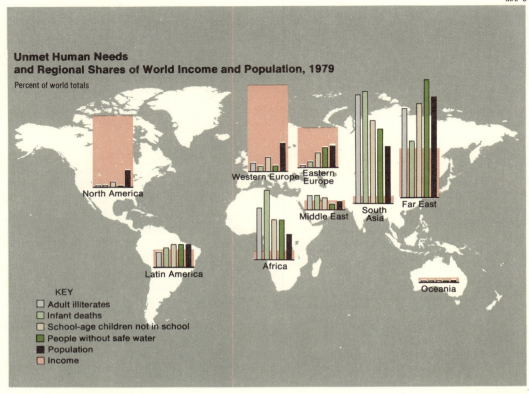

**Unmet Human Needs
and Regional Shares of World Income and Population, 1979**
Percent of world totals

KEY
☐ Adult illiterates
☐ Infant deaths
☐ School-age children not in school
■ People without safe water
■ Population
■ Income

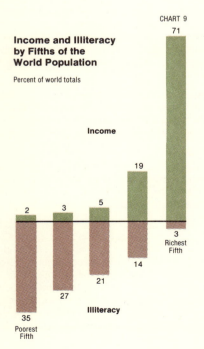

**Income and Illiteracy
by Fifths of the
World Population**

Percent of world totals

CHART 9

Income

Illiteracy

Third World countries are also relatively more affected by the diversion of labor and management skills to military programs and to the advanced technology that increasingly goes with them. They have fewer trained people to spare. Military requirements drain away talent essential for development. They may also introduce at too early a stage the complex technology that can be paralyzing for young countries.

Development in the poorer areas of the world has been slowed by another casualty of the arms race, foreign economic aid programs. For most of the donor countries, economic aid takes a low priority in competition with military expenditures. In 1980, according to OECD estimates, net economic aid amounted to $36 billion. This was equivalent to about 8 percent of the military outlays of the donors. Both superpowers fell below this average. US aid was equal to about 6 percent of its military expenditures, Soviet aid to about 1 percent.

Social Neglect

Lurking behind the impersonal statistics of income disparity is a tragedy of human deprivation almost beyond comprehension. The number of people in this earth who live in extreme poverty reaches into the hundreds of millions. The total may now be as high as one billion—that is, 1,000,000,000 individuals who live under such abysmal conditions that they lack the most basic necessities of life.

This is the ultimate immorality in a world able to lavish $600,000,000,000 in a single year on a military extravaganza.

Who are these terribly poor, the neglected members of world society, and where are they? Look around you. They can be found in the most developed countries in the world, eking out miserable lives in urban slums and rural backwaters. Areas of extreme poverty coexist with abundance. But most of the poorest, by far, are in the poorer countries (map 5). Perhaps one-tenth of them in Latin America, northern Africa, and the Middle East; the bulk of them in Asia and in sub-Saharan Africa. Large numbers are concentrated in India, Bangladesh, and Indonesia. The majority of the poor are rural dwellers. About two in five are children.

CHART 10

Food Consumption in Calories as a Percent of Requirements

national averages

Over-fed

+40-50%	Bulgaria, Czechoslovakia, Germany E., Ireland, Italy, Libya
+30-39%	Austria, Belgium, Denmark, France, Germany W. Greece, Hungary, Luxembourg, New Zealand, Poland, Portugal, Singapore, Spain, Switzerland, United Kingdom, United States, USSR, Yugoslavia
+20-29%	Argentina, Australia, Barbados, Canada, Cyprus, Gabon, Iran, Japan, Korea N., Korea S., Malta, Mexico, Netherlands, Norway, Paraguay, Romania
+10-19%	Albania, Chile, Costa Rica, Cuba, Egypt, Finland, Iceland, Iraq, Israel, Ivory Coast, Jamaica, Malaysia, Mauritius, Mongolia, Morocco, South Africa, Sweden, Syria, Trinidad & Tobago, Tunisia, Turkey
+1-9%	Burma, Cameroon, China, Colombia, Guyana, Indonesia, Lebanon, Lesotho, Liberia, Madagascar, Nicaragua, Philippines, Saudi Arabia, Sri Lanka, Sudan, Swaziland, Thailand, Uruguay, Venezuela
100%	Pakistan, Algeria, Benin
−1-9%	Botswana, Burundi, Central African Republic, Congo, Dominican Republic, Ecuador, El Salvador, Gambia, Guatemala, Honduras, Jordan, Malawi, Niger, Nigeria, Panama, Peru, Rwanda, Senegal, Sierra Leone, Somalia, Togo, Vietnam, Yemen A.R., Zaire
−10-19%	Angola, Bangladesh, Bolivia, Brazil, Cambodia, Ghana, Guinea, Haiti, India, Kenya, Laos, Mali, Mauritania, Mozambique, Nepal, Papua New Guinea, Tanzania, Upper Volta, Yemen P.D.R., Zambia
−20-29%	Afghanistan, Chad, Ethiopia, Uganda, Zimbabwe

Under-fed

The height of each segment of the bar indicates the size of the national populations falling within that average. From top to bottom the bar represents a global population of over 4 billion.

The usual benchmark of poverty is minimal income, but other inequalities go with it and make clear why the cycle of underdevelopment is so hard to break out of. One-third of the world lives in countries where the average caloric intake is below FAO's estimate of daily requirements (chart 10). The poor spend most of their income on food. Yet they live with daily hunger. Many are so malnourished that their ability to work is diminished. The malnutrition which restricts their productivity also weakens bodily resistance and sharply limits their life expectancy. Their children are susceptible to diseases that in richer settings are prevented by immunization. They have a much higher death rate in infancy, twenty times as high as babies born in families of upper incomes. Inadequately nourished, the children who survive in the world of poverty may grow up physically and mentally impaired. They are handicapped before they can become full members of society.

Illiteracy, like infant mortality, is disproportionately high among the poor (chart 9). The great majority of adults are illiterate. Of their children who attend school, less than half complete more than a year or two at the primary level. They go into adulthood lacking the basic reading skills which could improve their productivity as farmers, or possibly help them to function in a newly industrialized economy.

Locked in the dehumanizing desolation of hunger and illiteracy, the dispossessed of today's world are beginning to break out. More and more of them are on the move, as refugees to foreign lands or to more promising areas of their own countries. By the millions they are fleeing to cities in search of jobs and food. Their slums spill into the urban centers where their presence is a constant reminder of a festering wound which society must heal if it wishes to survive.

How can it be done? How can the burden of poverty be lifted from the backs of one billion people? And what, if anything, does the world's military mania have to do with it? One obvious approach, as the World Bank and other development authorities have long pointed out, is to make more accessible the services essential to people's health and productivity: basic education, clean water, preventive medical care, public utilities and transport. However, these are normally the responsibilities of governments and they must be paid for out of public budgets—budgets which are presently overburdened with the cost of large armies and military hardware. Here is one place to begin.

Like the other problems mentioned above (inflation, unemployment, income inequality), social neglect also calls for corrective adjustments even more basic than the reordering of budget priorities. Needed are policies that will stimulate the civilian economy through growth-producing research and investment; that will provide a more equitable sharing of the benefits of growth; and that will encourage the concerted international action so essential in today's interdependent world. The policies associated with an intense arms race do not further any of these objectives; in fact, they are counterproductive to all of them.

The times call for a new global vision. One which is less diverted by exaggerated military fantasies and more attuned to the realities of human needs. Fortunately there is no lack of ideas about how to get from here to there. The next section touches on a few of the proposals that have recently been raised in public forums.

"The test of our progress is not whether we add more to the abundance of those who have too much; it is whether we provide enough for those who have too little."

Franklin Delano Roosevelt
United States, 1937

Alternatives

CHART 11

Two Faces of World Security

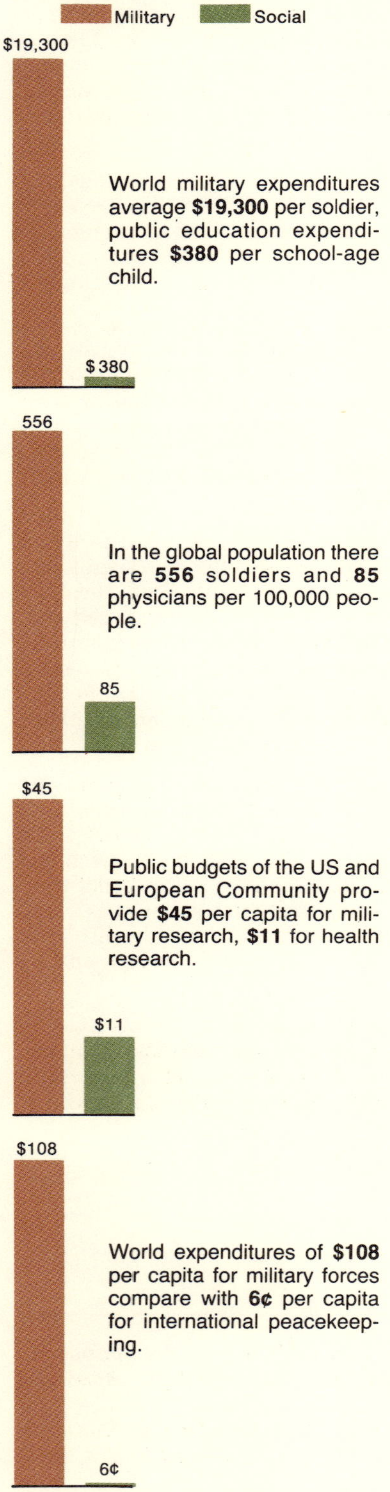

██ Military   ██ Social

$19,300

World military expenditures average **$19,300** per soldier, public education expenditures **$380** per school-age child.

$ 380

556

In the global population there are **556** soldiers and **85** physicians per 100,000 people.

85

$45

Public budgets of the US and European Community provide **$45** per capita for military research, **$11** for health research.

$11

$108

World expenditures of **$108** per capita for military forces compare with **6¢** per capita for international peacekeeping.

6¢

The pursuit of international security through national military force has been increasingly costly, in blood, money—and security. There are few who would deny that the weapons of mass destruction that have been created and the heavy burden imposed on society have further imperiled the world's safety and well-being.

A search for alternatives is not new; it has been in the minds and hearts of many thoughtful people since the birth of civilization. Now it has been given new impetus by at least two factors.

One is the increasing interdependence of world society. In physical, social, and economic terms, it has become a world without borders, wrapped in interlocking needs. None of its basic problems—the provision of food, clean water, and energy, the control of population growth, the preservation of natural resources needed for survival—stops at national borders. Not one can be solved by national miltary forces, no matter how powerful.

Awareness of this interdependence has spread particularly with the growing consciousness of worldwide environmental dangers. The economic shocks of recent years and the evident inadequacy of narrow national policies to cope with them have given it further impetus.

Another major development is the appearance of direct public participation in military issues. The scope of public debate today is a relatively new phenomenon. Traditionally military policy and decisions have been the province of government officials, joined by a few cognoscenti who kept the debate alive among themselves. Dialogue on security issues in any case has always been one-sided, since officials found it difficult to convey the facts, for "security" reasons, to the people who were footing the bills.

Furthermore, as the weaponry has become more complex so has the language. It has been made more so by inversions of meaning, eg: the recent major lift in the tempo of the arms race is announced as "Peace through strength"; the military command controlling the most powerful assembly of nuclear weapons on earth has as its motto "Peace is our profession".

It is only recently that the public has begun seriously to question whether this very expensive game of security is actually being played for their benefit. There have been critical mechanical failures in the most advanced and expensive technology. Now that the players are in control of limitless destructive power, could it be that there are dangerous human as well as mechanical weaknesses in the game that is being played?

What brought the west Europeans out into the streets, in massive marches of protest in virtually every major city, was an official decision to place more nuclear weapons in their own backyards. They suddenly saw themselves and all that they cherished as potential victims of a mindless system in which they had no role.

Components of a security system

The principal public activism so far has been directed at overt military activities that appear to imperil rather than ensure the public safety e.g. the emplacement of nuclear weapons, arms bazaars, civil defense measures against nuclear attack. Related to this is a widening interest in disarmament policies. Some of these will be discussed below.

An alternative international security system, however, has positive as well as negative (arms reduction) components, and these are equally essential to progress. Economic security is an important element of the system, with ramifications at least as fundamental as the political liberties that military defense is intended to protect. The freeing of resources for growth-producing economic purposes is recognized to be a major benefit of progress in disarmament, and a prime argument for it. Ideally, cooperation in constructive economic endeavors will reenforce a movement away from competition of a destructive nature, and the easing of economic strains will further strengthen the peace.

Mechanisms for deterring aggression, resolving disputes, and dealing with breaches of the peace are also critical components of an international security

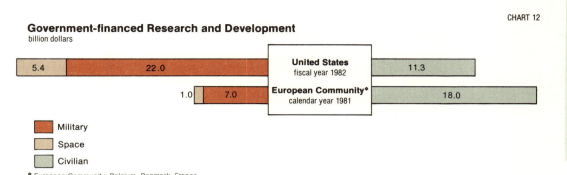

CHART 12

Government-financed Research and Development
billion dollars

| 5.4 | 22.0 | **United States** fiscal year 1982 | 11.3 |
| 1.0 | 7.0 | **European Community*** calendar year 1981 | 18.0 |

- ■ Military
- ■ Space
- ■ Civilian

* *European Community: Belgium, Denmark, France, Greece, Ireland, Italy, Netherlands, United Kingdom, West Germany.*

The Priorities are awry

As the arms race continues, contrasts between the military and social worlds have become more pronounced. Record outlays for arms and armies produce grotesque distortions of national priorities. Public expenditures have reached $19,300 per soldier, 50 times the average spent to educate a child of school age *(chart 11)*. In an intense competition for ever more destructive weaponry, the two superpowers (US and USSR) invest at least twice as much for research on military programs as for all civilian needs combined *(chart 12)*.

Increasingly apparent are the harsh consequences for the public welfare. Countries with the highest military burdens compete less effectively in world markets *(chart 13)*. The global economy suffers from wild inflation and record unemployment. Almost one-fourth of its inhabitants live in extreme poverty. Extravagant military defense has become the symbol of world *in*security.

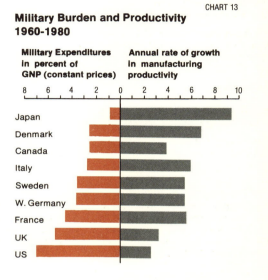

CHART 13

Military Burden and Productivity 1960-1980

Military Expenditures in percent of GNP (constant prices) | Annual rate of growth in manufacturing productivity

And the Public has begun to speak out

Three years ago a wave of public indignation began to gather momentum and roll over western Europe. And it has not stopped. It swept eastward across the Atlantic and the Americas and westward to the Pacific and Japan. Passing over eastern Europe and the Soviet Union, its tone was subdued but clearer than some might have supposed.

Ordinary people were rising up to say in largely polite, but insistent, voices that they wanted the nuclear genie put back into the bottle. And more than that, it developed, they wanted an end to the political atmosphere of suspicion and fear, and the beginning of a true commitment to peace.

The activism began with nuclear weapons—aroused by a new buildup in Europe and the official rationale that it was necessary to increase these weapons in order to reduce them through arms control. In 1982 the movement is broad both in scope and participation. It has two strong characteristics which give it a promising future:

—a constituency of unusual breadth, of all ages and economic groups, including nuclear physicists, churches, lawyers, labor unions, environmentalists, women's groups, and physicians.

—a determination to be heard not only on nuclear matters but on a range of issues formerly accepted as the esoteric province of government officials.

Some highlights of the peaceful demonstrations during the past year indicate how widely based geographically the movement has become:

In *Tokyo,* one of the largest anti-nuclear rallies ever held in Japan had 300,000 participants. At the UN session in June, the Japanese delegation presented an appeal against nuclear weapons signed by 30 million Japanese.

In *Israel,* during the invasion of Lebanon, 70,000 demonstrated for peace.

In *Sicily,* 80,000 marched in protest of proposed cruise missile bases.

In *USSR,* several hundred Scandinavian and Russian women marched quietly for peace from Leningrad to Minsk.

In *Romania,* which officially supports cuts in Warsaw Pact military expenditures, there were peace rallies in several cities.

In *Bonn* and *Amsterdam,* anti-nuclear rallies attracted more than 300,000.

In *Barcelona,* 75,000 Spaniards called for nuclear disarmament.

In *Athens,* 200,000 assembled to protest foreign military bases in Greece.

In *New York,* 600,000 turned out for peace, in the largest rally on a political issue ever recorded in the US.

Arms Control and Disarmament Agreements

The historical record of official negotiations on disarmament shows limited results so far. For more than three decades the major emphasis has been on nuclear weapons, but no agreement has yet been reached on the "discontinuance of all test explosions of nuclear weapons" (a pledge of the signers of the Partial Test Ban Treaty of 1963), nor on measures for the "cessation of the nuclear arms race" (a pledge of the signers of the NPT in 1968). Furthermore, the last three US-USSR treaties that were signed (SALT II and two nuclear test ban treaties) have not been ratified.

After a prolonged hiatus, new bilateral negotiations on nuclear disarmament have now begun. There are also talks on force reductions in Europe, and the 40-nation conference in Geneva will continue to pursue the elusive bans on chemical weapons and on all nuclear weapons tests.

Nuclear Weapons

To prevent the spread of nuclear weapons—

Antarctic Treaty, 1959   25 states[1]
Bans any military uses of Antarctica and specifically prohibits nuclear tests and nuclear waste.

Outer Space Treaty, 1967   81 states[1]
Bans nuclear weapons in earth orbit and their stationing in outer space.

Latin American Nuclear-Free Zone Treaty, 1967   22 states[1]
Bans testing, possession, deployment, of nuclear weapons and requires safeguards on facilities. All Latin American states except Argentina, Brazil, Chile, Cuba, are parties to the treaty.

Non-Proliferation Treaty, 1968   118 states[1]
Bans transfer of weapons or weapons technology to non-nuclear-weapons states. Requires safeguards on their facilities. Commits nuclear-weapon states to negotiations to halt the arms race.

Seabed Treaty, 1971   70 states[1]
Bans nuclear weapons on the seabed beyond a 12-mile coastal limit.

To reduce the risk of nuclear war—

Hot Line and Modernization Agreements, 1963   US—USSR
Establishes direct radio and wire-telegraph links between Moscow and Washington to ensure communication between heads of government in times of crisis. A second agreement in 1971 provided for satellite communication circuits.

Accidents Measures Agreement, 1971   US—USSR
Pledges US and USSR to improve safeguards against accidental or unauthorized use of nuclear weapons.

Prevention of Nuclear War Agreement, 1973   US—USSR
Requires consultation between the two countries if there is a danger of nuclear war.

To limit nuclear testing—

Partial Test Ban Treaty, 1963   111 states[1]
Bans nuclear weapons tests in the atmosphere, outer space, or underwater. Bans underground explosions which cause release of radioactive debris beyond the state's borders.

Threshhold Test Ban Treaty, 1974   US—USSR[2]
Bans underground tests having a yield above 150 kilotons (150,000 tons of TNT equivalent).

Peaceful Nuclear Explosions Treaty, 1974   US—USSR[2]
Bans "group explosions" with aggregate yield over 1,500 kilotons and requires on-site observers of group explosions with yield over 150 kilotons.

To limit nuclear weapons—

ABM Treaty (SALT I) and Protocol, 1972   US—USSR
Limits anti-ballistic missile systems to two deployment areas on each side. Subsequently, in Protocol of 1974, each side restricted to one deployment area.

SALT I Interim Agreement, 1972   US—USSR
Freezes the number of strategic ballistic misssile launchers, and permits an increase in SLBM launchers up to an agreed level only with equivalent dismantling of older ICBM or SLBM launchers.

SALT II, 1979   US—USSR[2]
Limits numbers of strategic nuclear delivery vehicles, launchers of Mirv'd missiles, bombers with long-range cruise missles, warheads on existing ICBM's, etc. Bans testing or deploying new ICBM's.

Other Weapons

To prohibit use of gas—

Geneva Protocol, 1925   113 states
Bans the use in war of asphyxiating, poisonous, or other gases, and of bacteriological methods of warfare.

To prohibit biological weapons—

Biological Weapons Convention, 1972   89 States
Bans the development, production, and stockpiling of biological and toxin weapons; requires the destruction of stocks.

To prohibit techniques changing the environment—

Environmental Modification Convention, 1977   31 states
Bans military or other hostile use of techniques to change weather or climate patterns, ocean currents, ozone layer, or ecological balance.

To control use of inhumane weapons—

Inhumane Weapons Convention, 1981   3 states[3]
Bans use of fragmentation bombs not detectable in the human body; bans use against civilians of mines, booby traps, and incendiary weapons; requires record-keeping on mines.

Other Candidates for Agreement

The list of problems awaiting agreement is much longer than the achievements to date. It includes conventional as well as nuclear and chemical weapons, and positive steps to *reduce* arms, rather than merely to control them. A few of the measures that have been discussed are listed below.

Comprehensive nuclear test ban
Nuclear weapons-free zones
Nuclear weapons freeze
Renunciation of first use of nuclear weapons
Prohibition on the use of nuclear weapons

Cut-off in production of fissile material
Ban on production of chemical weapons
Limitations of military expenditures
Reductions of conventional arms
Reductions of conventional forces
Registration of arms transfers
Ban on arms transfers to areas of conflict
Dismantling of foreign military bases
Comprehensive program of disarmament: a carefully planned structure, with time limits, encompassing the above and more.

1. Number of accessions and ratifications. 2. Not yet ratified. 3. Convention just opened to ratification this year.

system. Through the office of the UN Secretary-General and the International Court, machinery already exists. How it functions and what it has achieved are not widely known. With public support it could be strengthened to ensure that it is in fact used as it should be in times of crisis.

Disarmament

The 50th anniversary of the first world conference on disarmament has also been the occasion for the Second UN Special Session on Disarmament. With public marches and convocations as well, it has been a year of banner headlines for peace and disarmament. Unfortunately the political results have been nowhere near the level of public concern and expectation.

Years of painstaking negotiations and more than a dozen international agreements have seemed to have no appreciable effect on the pace of the arms race. They may have discouraged some activities (eg. a faster spread of nuclear weapons) and possibly curbed areas of future development (eg. the antarctic, the seabeds). They have not put a cap on military expansion. Although disarmament negotiations are to continue, the prospects for any significant breakthrough in the normal course of diplomatic meetings are at present considered to be dim.

It is under these conditions that public activism has taken on new importance. Not only is there more of it but it is more desperately needed. It is a sign of the times that the one achievement of the officials gathered at the UN Special Session was an agreement on a world campaign for disarmament. It was as though they were reaching out to the public to be rescued from the slough of despond into which they had cast themselves. Educating the public has become the one last hope.

It is already clear that what the public can contribute is some simplification of a process that has become so ponderous and unwieldy that it can barely budge. There has already been a good harvest of straightforward suggestions. In these paragraphs there is room only for a few examples. They may give encouragement to others.

How do we simplify? One disarmament proposal is already on a number of US ballots, giving one voter in four a chance to vote on it this fall. The idea is simply to freeze nuclear weapons as they are. This means no further testing, production, or deployment. All verifiable, all fair. The argument it gets is that the opponent is "ahead". The answer: when nuclear overkill is so vast, the concept of balance between two adversaries is meaningless. The ability to kill fifty times over is no more of a deterrent than the ability to kill just once. Dead has no superlatives.

As for the nuclear reduction process, that can begin, as Professor Kennan suggested last year, with a clean 50 percent cut. Admiral Noel Gaylor has contributed to that a simple and verifiable procedure for achieving the cuts: let each side turn in to a referee an equal number of explosive nuclear fission devices. Each side choses the devices it wants to give up. Under supervision they are converted to power plant fuel. The reduction can be fast and the cuts very deep.

Simplification has many candidates. Nuclear-free zones can be simpler to arrange than comprehensive agreements. The idea of a Nordic area zone is still very much alive. There have been national or area proposals in Canada, New Zealand, India, the two Germanys, and widely in Europe. Wales is the first nuclear-free country. Size is no requirement. Even townships are making declarations. Enough towns can make a county, then a state, a nation, maybe a region, nuclear-free.

There are also the unlimited possibilities of informal reciprocal actions. Taking its cues from the escalation process, arms reduction can proceed the same way: each step carefully guided by the response the adversary makes. Mutual example is an accepted feature of disarmament policy even in these confrontational days. The two superpowers are observing three nuclear treaties that they have not ratified but are willing to abide by as long as the other nation does too.

In short, out of a bleak period for global security may come the impetus for major constructive change. If an awakened public continues to make its views known, we can expect a new approach to security. After all,

"The right to survive is the overriding priority". *   □

Pugwash Council, Canada, September 1981

"Virtually all the significant social and political movements in the last two decades have begun from below. Whether one speaks about liberation movements, or trade union movements, or the women's movement, or the environmental movement, all came up from below. And now we have the peace movement".
Soedjatmoko
Rector, United Nations University,1982

STATISTICAL ANNEX

The statistics which follow have been assembled for the purpose of analyzing comparative progress on a broad front, primarily for the world as a whole or for groups of countries. It is believed that they are representative for this purpose.

Because of the interest in the national figures which make up these totals, we are showing them in full detail for 1979 (Tables II and III). It cannot be emphasized too strongly that caution must be exercised in drawing conclusions from individual national figures, and particularly in making comparisons between countries. Some of the reasons why this is so are outlined in the statistical notes following.

Table III shows the country rank order on a per capita basis for military expenditures and social indicators. It is hoped that the selection is large enough to offset some of the inconsistencies in the individual series and to convey a general impression of relative standing.

MILITARY AND SOCIAL TRENDS
World, Developed,[1] and Developed[2] Countries, 1960-1980

TABLE I

	1960	1961	1962	1963	1964	1965	1966	1967	1968	1969	1970	1971	1972	1973	1974	1975	1976	1977	1978	1979	1980
Military Expenditures																					
billion US $																					
World[4]	100	102	114	119	121	126	140	159	170	178	183	190	209	233	272	309	330	369	420	478	541
Developed	90	92	103	106	107	109	122	140	149	155	156	160	176	194	220	244	255	285	321	366	424
Developing[4]	10	10	11	13	14	17	18	19	21	23	27	30	33	39	52	65	75	84	99	112	117
billion 1979 US $[3]																					
World[4]	298	301	329	336	333	337	361	401	417	419	411	401	411	411	428	436	448	458	463	478	495
Developed	270	272	297	299	295	291	314	351	363	363	347	334	342	340	349	345	348	355	352	366	389
Developing[4]	28	29	32	37	38	46	47	50	54	56	64	67	69	71	79	91	100	103	111	112	106
Arms Exports																					
billion US $																					
World	na	2.4	3.8	3.2	3.2	3.8	4.7	5.1	5.3	5.9	5.8	6.4	10.4	13.2	11.8	12.8	16.6	19.7	22.3	25.3	26.1
Developed	na	2.3	3.7	3.1	3.1	3.6	4.5	4.9	5.1	5.7	5.6	6.1	9.5	12.9	11.5	12.2	15.8	18.8	21.2	24.2	24.4
Developing	na	.1	.1	.1	.1	.2	.2	.2	.2	.2	.2	.2	.3	.9	.3	.3	.6	.8	.9	1.0	1.7
Arms Import																					
billion US $																					
World	na	2.4	3.8	3.2	3.2	3.8	4.7	5.1	5.3	5.9	5.8	6.4	10.4	13.2	11.8	12.8	16.6	19.7	22.3	25.3	26.1
Developed	na	1.3	1.7	1.6	1.8	1.7	1.5	1.7	1.7	2.2	2.1	2.1	3.2	3.9	4.5	4.3	5.3	5.4	5.5	5.7	6.6
Developing	na	1.1	2.1	1.6	1.4	2.1	3.2	3.4	3.6	3.7	3.9	4.3	7.2	9.3	7.3	8.5	11.3	14.3	16.8	19.6	19.5
Foreign Economic Aid																					
billion US $																					
World	5.2	5.8	6.1	6.4	6.6	6.6	7.0	7.7	7.4	7.8	8.3	9.4	10.3	12.3	16.2	21.1	21.2	23.1	25.2	30.5	35.9
Developed	5.0	5.6	5.9	6.2	6.4	6.4	6.8	7.4	7.2	7.5	7.6	8.4	9.3	10.6	12.4	15.3	15.3	17.0	21.2	24.3	28.6
Developing	.2	.2	.2	.2	.2	.2	.2	.3	.2	.3	.7	1.0	1.0	1.7	3.8	5.8	5.9	6.1	4.0	6.2	7.3
GNP																					
billion US $																					
World[5]	1,477	1,550	1,658	1,785	1,954	2,112	2,307	2,454	2,663	2,924	3,236	3,595	4,058	4,867	5,588	6,312	6,902	7,866	9,247	10,522	11,795
Developed	1,195	1,273	1,366	1,458	1,588	1,719	1,876	2,007	2,182	2,381	2,612	2,897	3,281	3,872	4,332	4,877	5,318	6,045	7,164	8,083	8,990
Developing[4]	282	277	292	3327	366	393	431	447	481	543	624	698	777	994	1,256	1,435	1,584	1,821	2,083	2,439	2,805
billion 1979 US $[3]																					
World[5]	4,380	4,560	4,770	5,043	5,376	5,656	5,971	6,197	6,555	6,896	7,289	7,616	8,014	8,601	8,787	8,905	9,375	9,772	10,199	10,522	10,792
Developed	3,584	3,760	3,933	4,109	4,371	4,590	4,838	5,030	5,318	5,571	5,813	6,049	6,381	6,800	6,871	6,895	7,263	7,534	7,852	8,083	8,248
Developing[5]	796	800	837	934	1,005	1,066	1,133	1,167	1,237	1,325	1,476	1,567	1,633	1,801	1,916	2,010	2,112	2,238	2,347	2,439	2,544
GNP per capita																					
US $																					
World[5]	485	501	528	555	598	632	676	704	748	804	872	948	1,049	1,234	1,390	1,541	1,654	1,851	2,138	2,395	2,633
Developed	1,359	1,430	1,515	1,597	1,720	1,842	1,992	2,111	2,275	2,460	2,673	2,938	3,294	3,858	4,277	4,782	5,173	5,835	6,875	7,698	8,505
Developing[5]	130	126	130	142	156	163	174	176	185	204	228	249	271	338	417	466	504	567	634	730	820
1979 US $[3]																					
World[5]	1,437	1,474	1,519	1,568	1,644	1,692	1,749	1,777	1,841	1,897	1,964	2,010	2,072	2,180	2,185	2,174	2,246	2,300	2,358	2,395	2,409
Developed	4,077	4,225	4,360	4,501	4,735	4,920	5,136	5,289	5,546	5,755	5,950	6,135	6,047	6,772	6,783	6,760	7,066	7,272	7,536	7,698	7,803
Developing[5]	367	363	374	405	428	442	458	460	475	497	540	559	569	612	636	653	671	696	714	730	743
Population																					
millions																					
World	3,047	3,093	3,141	3,217	3,269	3,343	3,414	3,487	3,561	3,635	3,712	3,790	3,867	3,944	4,021	4,097	4,173	4,249	4,325	4,402	4,479
Developed	879	890	902	913	923	933	942	951	959	968	977	986	996	1,004	1,013	1,020	1,028	1,036	1,042	1,050	1,057
Developing	2,168	2,203	2,239	2,304	2,346	2,410	2,472	2,536	2,602	2,667	2,735	2,804	2,871	2,940	3,009	3,077	3,145	3,213	3,283	3,352	3,422
Armed Forces																					
thousands																					
World	18,550	18,960	19,525	19,441	19,771	19,528	19,886	20,843	21,408	21,622	21,484	21,685	21,396	21,739	21,996	21,863	22,364	23,181	23,818	24,466	24,642
Developed	9,851	10,056	10,400	10,018	9,981	9,711	10,132	10,503	10,600	10,628	10,146	9,835	9,561	9,513	9,561	9,550	9,511	9,516	9,485	9,502	9,538
Developing	8,699	8,904	9,125	9,423	9,790	9,817	9,754	10,340	10,808	10,994	11,338	11,850	11,835	12,226	12,435	12,313	12,853	13,665	14,333	14,964	15,104
Physicians																					
thousands																					
World	1,668	1,723	1,780	1,836	1,913	1,977	2,039	2.145	2,175	2,253	2,317	2,400	2,520	2,630	2,709	2,802	3,198	3,332	3,438	3,722	na
Developed	1.226	1,265	1,303	1,342	1,396	1,428	1,473	1,554	1,564	1,610	1,658	1,717	1,792	1,860	1,915	1,982	2,145	2,228	2,274	2,439	na
Developing	442	458	477	494	517	549	566	591	611	643	659	683	728	770	794	820	1,054	1,104	1,164	1,283	na
Teachers																					
thousands																					
World	14,526	15,169	15,956	16,781	17,603	18,150	18,814	19,631	20,295	21,165	22,129	22,727	23,655	24,485	25,140	25,890	26,673	27,518	28,371	31,087[6]	31,930[7]
Developed	6,580	6,814	7,056	7,340	7,632	7,908	8,084	8,274	8,560	8,667	8,823	8,945	9,062	9,265	9,446	9,467	9,524	9,571	9,647	9,680	9,730[7]
Developing	7,946	8,355	8,900	9,441	9,971	10,242	10,730	11,357	11,735	12,498	13,306	13,782	14,593	15,220	15,694	16,423	17,149	17,947	18,724	21,407[6]	22,200[7]

na not available

1. *Developed countries,* 28 in number, are those identified by an asterisk in Tables II and III. They include countries listed in North America, most of Europe, Oceania, Israel, and Japan.
2. *Developing countries.* 113 in number, are the countries listed in Latin America, seven in Europe (Albania, Greece, Malta, Portugal, Spain, Turkey, and Yugoslavia), Asia except Israel and Japan, all of Africa, Fiji and Papua New Guinea in Oceania.
3. Values expressed in 1979 prices and converted to dollars at 1979 exchange rates.
4. Not including Cambodia after 1975.
5. Not including Lebanon or Cambodia.
6. Sharp increase 1978 to 1979 reflects inauguration of reporting by China.
7. Projected.

COMPARATIVE RESOURCES
141 Countries, 1979

TABLE II

	Population		Area			GNP	PUBLIC EXPENDITURES						HUMAN RESOURCES		
							Military		Int'l. Peace-keeping	Education	Health	Foreign Economic Aid	Armed Forces	Physicians	Teachers
	1,000	% Urban	1,000 sq. km.	% Arable¹	Density²	million US $	million US $	% of GNP	million US $³	million US $	million US $	million US $	1,000	1,000	1,000
WORLD	**4,401,721**	**41**	**132,122**	**11**	**33**	**10,522,143**	**477,978**	**4.5**	**244**	**545,882**	**373,540**	**30,523**	**24,466**	**3,722.5**	**31,087**
Developed*	1,049,687	71	53,948	11	19	8,083,086	365,592	4.5	239	456,728	336,213	24,280	9,502	2,439.2	9,680
Developing	3,352,034	32	78,174	11	43	2,439,057	112,386	4.6	5	89,154	37,327	6,243	14,964	1,283.3	21,407
AMERICA															
North America	**248,745**	**74**	**19,339**	**12**	**13**	**2,595,974**	**126,399**	**4.9**	**94**	**169,148**	**97,208**	**5,710**	**2,102**	**460.5**	**2,709**
United States*	225,055	74	9,363	20	24	2,375,200	122,279	5.2	74	152,200	86,300	4,684	2,022	417.3	2,451
Canada*	23,690	76	9,976	4	2	220,774	4,120	1.9	20	16,948	10,908	1,026	80	43.2	258
Latin America	**347,782**	**61**	**20,231**	**8**	**17**	**574,092**	**7,812**	**1.4**	**2**	**21,915**	**8,070**	**83**	**1,181**	**246.1**	**2,852**
Argentina	27,226	80	2,767	13	10	60,350	1,497	2.5	.623	2,050	278	—	133	51.0	266
Barbados	279	44	0.4	77	698	648	2	.3	.004	43	20	—	1	.2	3
Bolivia	5,213	34	1,099	3	5	2,960	96	3.2	.001	105	31	—	23	2.7	53
Brazil	119,175	61	8,512	7	14	213,537	1,687	.8	.521	7,658	3,430	—	281	68.0	983
Chile	10,848	80	757	7	14	20,660	956	4.6	.044	764	458	—	85	6.6	84
Colombia	24,592	60	1,139	5	22	27,859	212	.8	.032	502	362	—	68	12.9	198
Costa Rica	2,184	41	51	10	43	3,530	—	—	.008	201	42	—	—	1.5	18
Cuba	9,824	64	114	28	86	13,920	778	5.6	.063	1,200	445	—	189	13.5	148
Dominican Rep.	5,551	49	49	25	114	5,321	100	1.9	.003	132	99	—	19	2.7	31
Ecuador	7,763	43	284	9	27	8,874	185	2.1	.010	335	83	—	33	4.8	63
El Salvador	4,662	39	21	34	222	3,469	48	1.4	.003	111	44	—	7	1.4	20
Guatemala	6,849	36	109	17	63	6,863	85	1.2	.003	131	60	—	18	2.6	27
Guyana	832	40	215	2	4	487	16	3.3	.001	48	12	—	5	.2	8
Haiti	5,670	24	28	32	204	1,121	16	1.4	.002	20	9	—	7	.6	17
Honduras	3,635	31	112	16	32	2,057	50	2.4	.004	72	35	—	11	1.1	18
Jamaica	2,234	41	11	24	203	2,256	20	.9	.016	160	72	—	4	.8	20
Mexico	66,140	65	1,972	12	34	117,664	633	.5	.392	5,265	863	—	100	38.0	566
Nicaragua	2,365	49	130	12	18	1,517	54	3.6	.001	45	24	—	8	1.5	12
Panama	1,840	51	76	7	24	2,761	15	.5	.005	137	129	—	11	1.6	18
Paraguay	3,117	40	407	3	8	3,383	42	1.2	.001	44	15	—	15	1.7	27
Peru	17,149	62	1,285	3	13	14,534	435	3.0	.008	344	134	—	92	11.7	114
Trinidad & Tobago	1,150	49	5	31	225	4,448	15	.3	.015	178	97	—	1	.8	8
Uruguay	2,910	83	176	11	16	6,944	173	2.5	.015	139	69	—	28	5.4	23
Venezuela	16,574	75	912	4	18	48,929	697	1.4	.253	2,231	1,259	83	42	14.8	127
EUROPE															
NATO Europe⁴	**325,151**	**72**	**2,890**	**30**	**112**	**2,562,261**	**91,731**	**3.6**	**85**	**129,838**	**134,374**	**12,010**	**2,780**	**617.8**	**2,915**
Belgium*	9,849	95	30	26	323	110,542	3,630	3.3	2	6,576	4,470	631	87	24.0	88
Denmark*	5,118	67	43	62	119	63,774	1,518	2.4	2	4,040	4,210	448	35	10.6	60
France*	53,477	73	547	35	98	574,481	22,663	3.9	17	29,940	35,000	3,370	509	96.0	537
Germany, West*	61,337	92	249	30	247	764,509	24,796	3.2	15	34,726	41,500	3,350	495	135.7	503
Greece	9,444	65	132	30	72	39,809	2,424	6.1	1	977	1,154	—	185	22.3	63
Iceland*	226	87	103	—	2	2,389	—	—	.066	86	136	—	—	.5	3
Italy*	56,888	67	301	41	189	322,962	7,762	2.4	7	14,736	14,919	273	365	164.6	575
Luxembourg*	358	68	3	26	138	4,921	42	.8	.085	296	40	na	1	.5	3
Netherlands*	14,030	88	41	23	344	149,553	5,043	3.4	3	11,925	9,690	1,404	115	24.9	111
Norway*	4,074	44	324	2	12	44,485	1,454	3.3	1	3,491	2,936	429	39	7.8	47
Portugal	9,843	29	92	39	107	19,422	687	3.5	.185	742	622	—	60	18.1	81
Turkey	44,561	45	781	36	57	61,814	2.556	4.1	.156	2,148	480	—	566	26.0	255
United Kingdom*	55,946	78	244	28	229	403,600	19,156	4.8	37	20,155	19,217	2,105	323	86.8	589
ALL NATO (incl. US and canada)	**573,896**	**73**	**22,229**	**14**	**26**	**5,158,235**	**218,130**	**4.2**	**179**	**298,986**	**231,582**	**17,720**	**4,882**	**1,078.3**	**5,624**
Warsaw Pact	**372,183**	**61**	**23,393**	**12**	**16**	**1,538,160**	**127,460**	**8.3**	**20**	**71,170**	**38,620**	**1,852**	**4,764**	**1,174.8**	**3,010**
Bulgaria*	8,827	60	111	38	80	32,470	940	2.9	.019	1,180	650		150	21.0	58
Czechoslovakia*	15,182	67	128	41	119	79,140	2,250	2.8	1	2,440	2,300		194	41.0	99
Germany, East*	16,745	76	108	46	155	106,370	3,930	3.7	1	4,170	4,200		159	33.5	111
Hungary*	10,699	52	93	58	115	40,540	1,020	2.5	.045	1,790	1,180	} 420	104	26.0	80
Poland*	35,257	57	313	48	113	133,450	3,900	2.9	.191	3,940	4,470		318	61.5	215
Romania*	22,048	48	238	44	93	78,900	1,420	1.8	.033	2,340	1,820		181	31.3	159
USSR*	263,425	62	22,402	10	12	1,067,290	114,000	10.7	18	55,310	24,000	1,432	3,658	960.5	2,288

	Population		Area			GNP	Military		PUBLIC EXPENDITURES Int'l. Peace-keeping	Education	Health	Foreign Economic Aid	HUMAN RESOURCES Armed Forces	Physicians	Teachers
	1,000	% Urban	1,000 sq. km.	% Arable[1]	Density[2]	million US $	million US $	% of GNP	million US $[3]	million US $	million US $	million US $	1,000	1,000	1,000
Other Europe	**92,515**	**59**	**1,772**	**21**	**52**	**574,866**	**12,930**	**2.2**	**18**	**28,732**	**26,043**	**1,412**	**801**	**177.9**	**775**
Albania	2,626	34	29	23	91	2,244	180	8.0	.250	90	65	—	43	2.8	27
Austria*	7,506	52	84	19	90	67,988	836	1.2	5	3,834	3,399	127	38	18.0	72
Finland*	4,764	59	337	7	14	40,760	599	1.5	1	2,320	1,623	86	40	8.5	39
Ireland*	3,365	52	70	14	48	14,746	205	1.4	.438	1,008	885	na	14	4.2	32
Malta	347	94	0.3	44	1,157	918	11	1.2	.006	30	30	—	1	.4	3
Spain	37,108	70	505	41	74	195,846	3,512	1.8	.210	4,087	5,600	na	321	81.7	301
Sweden*	8,296	83	450	7	18	100,856	3,383	3.4	3	9,656	7,665	956	66	17.5	97
Switzerland*	6,343	55	41	10	154	99,098	2,056	2.1	8	5,003	3,963	207	19	14.8	38
Yugoslavia	22,160	39	256	31	87	52,410	2,148	4.1	.060	2,704	2,813	36	259	30.0	166
ASIA															
Middle East	**130,154**	**47**	**6,411**	**6**	**20**	**293,675**	**38,731**	**13.2**	**1**	**14,873**	**4,642**	**5,625**	**1,461**	**95.3**	**952**
Bahrain	370	78	0.6	3	617	2,032	141	6.9	.006	69	49	—	2	.3	3
Cyprus	621	53	9	47	68	1,782	35	2.0	.306	60	27	—	10	.6	5
Egypt[5]	40,891	44	1,001	3	41	18,874	1,865	9.9	.053	772	283	—	395	42.0	224
Iran	37,647	47	1,648	10	23	73,258	4,489	6.1	.110	4,180	1,309	25	200	16.2	272
Iraq	12,701	66	435	12	29	33,438	2,675	8.0	.016	1,066	267	847	222	6.4	121
Israel*	3,783	87	21	20	182	18,601	5,540	29.8	.126	1,470	722	8	166	10.2	57
Jordan	3,189	42	98	14	33	2,701	382	14.1	.005	168	61	—	67	1.4	25
Kuwait	1,277	56	18	—	72	25,780	900	3.5	.124	691	369	1,055	11	2.0	22
Lebanon	2,943	60	10	33	283	na	228	na	.007	na	na	—	9	5.0	38
Oman	864	5	212	—	4	2,994	779	26.0	.006	81	52	—	19	.5	5
Qatar	210	69	11	—	19	4,710	1,000	21.2	.007	560	na	277	5	.2	3
Saudi Arabia	9,292	24	2,150	—	4	76,239	17,068	22.4	.134	4,842	1,140	2,298	44	5.2	70
Syria	8,506	49	185	31	46	10,078	2,024	20.1	.003	584	40	—	228	3.6	79
United Arab Emirates	871	65	84	—	10	18,984	1,151	6.1	.010	197	285	1,115	25	1.0	8
Yemen, Arab Rep.	5,126	11	195	14	26	3,341	350	10.5	.001	94	30	—	37	.5	10
Yemen, Peoples Dem. Rep.	1,863	33	333	1	6	863	104	12.0	.001	39	8	—	21	.2	10
South Asia	**892,350**	**28**	**5,091**	**42**	**175**	**172,341**	**5,159**	**3.0**	**.457**	**5,005**	**1,873**	**—**	**1.725**	**213.5**	**3,747**
Afghanistan	15,913	11	648	12	24	3,770	64	1.7	.002	71	23	—	90	1.0	38
Bangladesh	86,128	9	144	63	598	9,423	129	1.4	.010	144	35	—	76	7.9	297
India	677,028	21	3,288	52	206	133,270	3,870	2.9	.397	4,269	1,600	na	1,096	180.0	2,988
Nepal	14,608	4	141	16	104	1,794	16	.9	.003	29	13	—	20	.4	40
Pakistan	84,063	26	804	25	104	20,762	1,054	5.1	.036	415	125	—	429	22.0	265
Sri Lanka	14,610	22	66	33	223	3,322	26	.8	.009	77	77	—	14	2.2	119
Far East	**1,557,824**	**30**	**16,387**	**11**	**95**	**1,762,092**	**54,462**	**3.1**	**18**	**82,871**	**53,515**	**2,737**	**8,394**	**655.3**	**12,192**
Brunei	213	64	6	2	37	2,206	172	7.8	—	49	na	—	3	.1	3
Burma	33,590	24	677	15	50	5,093	189	3.7	.006	82	50	—	170	7.0	98
Cambodia	5,767	12	181	17	32	na	na	na	.001	na	na	—	30	.1	26
China	1,012,197	26	9,597	10	105	480,000	32,000	6.7	.117	16,000	7,200	100	4,360	400.0	8,460
Indonesia	148,085	18	2,027	10	73	47,213	1,711	3.6	.041	944	552	—	239	12.4	1,022
Japan*	115,870	76	372	13	311	1,019,360	9,632	.9	18	58,821	43,800	2,637	241	148.6	907
Korea, North	17,473	33	120	18	145	19,716	1,230	6.2	—	590	50	—	672	7.0	100
Korea, South	39,144	48	98	22	397	61,051	3,354	5.5	—	2,055	122	—	619	21.0	197
Laos	3,440	15	237	4	14	340	35	10.3	.001	na	3	—	49	.2	18
Malaysia	13,674	27	330	13	41	19,566	779	4.0	.053	1,122	304	—	64	1.8	107
Mongolia	1,616	47	1,565	1	1	1,268	130	10.2	.003	80	18	—	30	3.5	14
Philippines	47,820	32	300	33	159	29,826	641	2.2	.059	575	167	—	103	16.7	323
Singapore	2,363	100	0.6	14	3,938	8,933	458	5.1	.047	256	132	—	36	1.9	16
Taiwan	17,459	77	32	na	540	32,246	2,105	6.5	—	1,150	838	—	539	19.4	123
Thailand	46,687	13	514	35	91	26,774	1,126	4.2	.048	847	211	—	216	6.4	404
Vietnam	52,426	19	330	18	159	8,500	900	10.6	.004	300	68	—	1,023	9.2	374
OCEANIA	**21,214**	**74**	**8,436**	**5**	**2**	**149,547**	**3,458**	**2.3**	**5**	**8,484**	**6,289**	**687**	**87**	**31.2**	**220**
Australia*	14,422	86	7,687	6	2	125,461	3,072	2.4	4	7,284	5,054	620	70	26.1	166
Fiji	618	37	18	13	34	997	10	1.0	.007	53	22	—	1	.3	6
New Zealand*	3,107	83	269	2	12	20,866	346	1.7	.638	1,043	1,156	67	13	4.6	37
Papua New Guinea	3,067	13	462	1	7	2,223	30	1.4	.002	104	57	—	3	.2	11

	Population		Area			GNP	Military		Int'l. Peace-keeping	Education	Health	Foreign Economic Aid	Armed Forces	Physicians	Teachers
							PUBLIC EXPENDITURES						**HUMAN RESOURCES**		
	1,000	% Urban	1,000 sq. km.	% Arable[1]	Density[2]	million US $	million US $	% of GNP	million US $[3]	million US $	million US $	million US $	1,000	1,000	1,000
AFRICA	413,803	24	28,172	6	15	299,135	9,836	3.3	.309	13.846	2,906	407	1,171	50.1	1,715
Algeria	18,256	55	2,382	3	8	31,218	602	1.9	.014	2,387	406	272	89	5.0	121
Angola	6,543	22	1,247	3	5	4,728	—	—	.010	109	47	—	40	.4	40
Benin	3,379	14	113	16	30	953	16	1.7	.001	46	13	—	2	.2	8
Botswana	769	12	600	2	1	531	27	5.1	.004	45	12	—	1	.1	6
Burundi	4,192	5	28	46	151	798	25	3.1	.001	23	8	—	5	.1	5
Cameroon	8.323	29	475	14	18	5,062	88	1.7	.003	155	39	—	8	.6	31
Central African Republic	2,284	42	623	3	4	619	14	2.3	.001	27	9	—	1	.1	5
Chad	4,528	18	1,284	2	4	558	40	7.2	.001	14	6	—	5	.1	5
Congo	1,508	39	342	2	4	1,053	52	4.9	.001	84	34	—	7	.3	10
Equatorial Guinea	244	51	28	8	9	147	6	4.1	.001	na	na	—	2	—	1
Ethiopia	29,977	13	1,222	11	24	3,937	349	8.9	.006	83	48	—	222	.5	40
Gabon	637	32	268	2	2	2,586	69	2.7	.001	96	41	—	2	.2	4
Gambia	585	16	11	23	52	126	—	—	.003	9	5	—	—	.1	2
Ghana	11,742	36	238	12	49	4,470	60	1.3	.010	136	52	—	20	1.5	80
Guinea	5,275	23	246	6	22	1,443	—	—	.001	62	17	—	9	.3	10
Ivory Coast	7,761	32	322	12	24	8,790	98	1.1	.003	752	141	—	5	.5	31
Kenya	15,778	10	583	4	27	5,881	291	5.0	.005	359	116	—	12	1.5	107
Lesotho	1,305	4	30	10	43	469	—	—	.002	11	6	—	1	.1	6
Liberia	1,839	29	111	3	16	939	13	1.4	.001	53	21	—	5	.2	8
Libya	2,920	60	1,760	1	2	23,249	500	2.2	.003	1,045	307	105	42	4.0	46
Madagascar	8,349	16	587	5	14	2,767	82	3.0	.004	139	61	—	11	.8	31
Malawi	5,862	9	118	19	49	1,279	47	3.7	.002	30	14	—	5	.1	12
Mali	6,464	17	1,240	2	5	1,268	37	2.9	.001	54	12	—	4	.3	10
Mauritania	1,474	23	1,031	—	1	488	70	14.3	.001	25	7	—	9	.1	2
Mauritius	941	44	2	58	470	1,019	2	.2	.002	64	27	—	na	.4	10
Morocco	20,368	42	447	17	46	15,479	896	5.8	.029	994	170	—	98	1.8	87
Mozambique	11,839	8	802	4	15	3,725	114	3.1	.003	37	na	—	24	.3	19
Niger	5,346	11	1,267	2	4	1,547	12	.8	.004	66	14	—	2	.1	6
Nigeria	74,595	20	924	33	81	75,369	1,991	2.6	.103	2,575	377	30	193	6.6	339
Rwanda	4,955	4	26	37	188	959	18	1.9	.002	25	7	—	4	.2	10
Senegal	5,532	32	196	26	28	2,524	59	2.3	.003	100	28	—	8	.4	13
Sierra Leone	3,309	16	72	24	46	865	8	.9	.001	35	10	—	3	.2	11
Somalia	3,474	31	638	2	5	1,351	95	7.0	.001	25	12	—	46	.3	10
South Africa	27,967	48	1,221	12	23	52,633	2,269	4.3	.058	2,263	210	—	63	13.6	173
Sudan	18,155	20	2,506	5	7	6,124	199	3.2	.004	319	62	—	63	2.2	58
Swaziland	541	8	17	9	31	353	10	2.8	.001	21	7	—	1	.1	4
Tanzania	18,018	13	945	5	19	4,561	267	5.8	.001	260	91	—	52	1.0	80
Togo	2,544	15	57	25	45	991	23	2.3	.003	60	22	—	3	.1	12
Tunisia	6,312	50	164	30	38	7.234	363	5.0	.003	426	157	—	22	1.5	35
Uganda	12,418	7	236	24	53	5,730	161	2.8	.002	117	63	—	21	.5	40
Upper Volta	6,661	5	274	9	24	1,010	32	3.2	.001	35	9	—	4	.1	4
Zaire	27,931	30	2.345	3	12	7,419	110	1.5	.005	372	76	—	21	1.9	133
Zambia	5,649	39	753	7	8	3,083	294	9.5	.003	145	70	—	14	.7	24
Zimbabwe	7,254	20	391	6	18	3,800	427	11.2	—	163	72	—	22	1.0	26

* Developed country
— None or negligible   na   not available
1. Includes permanent cropland, land under temporary crops, and land temporarily fallow.
2. Population per square kilometer of surface area.
3. Because peacekeeping expenditures have been relatively small, they are listed in fractions of millions of dollars in order to show the maximum number of national contributors. National and regional totals are rounded to millions if they are $1 million or higher.
4. Spain became a member of NATO in May 1982 and will be shown in NATO Europe beginning with data for that year.
5. Egypt is shown with the political grouping of Middle East states, rather than in Africa.

RANKING OF COUNTRIES, MILITARY AND SOCIAL INDICATORS

	MILITARY Public Expenditures per Capita		MILITARY Public Expenditures per Soldier[1]		MILITARY Public Expenditures per Sq. Km.		GNP Economic-Social Standing[2]	GNP per Capita		EDUCATION Public Expenditures per Capita		School-Age Population per Teacher[3]		% School-Age Population in School		% Women in Total University Enrollment		Literacy Rate[4]	
	Rank	US$	Rank	US$	Rank	US$	Avg. Rank	Rank	US$	Rank	US$	Rank	Number	Rank	Number	Rank	%	Rank	%
WORLD		108		19,536		3,618			2,395		124		46		54		40		70
Developed		348		38,475		6,777			7,698		435		26		70		44		99
Developing		34		7,510		1,438			730		27		56		51		33		59
AMERICA																			
North America		508		60,133		6,536			10,436		680		23		83		47		99
United States*	8	543	6	60,474	25	13,060	7	14	10,554	9	676	10	23	2	84	17	47	1	99
Canada*	26	174	9	51,500	88	413	8	16	9,319	8	715	15	24	5	75	14	48	22	98
Latin America		23		6,615		386			1,651		63		44		58		36		79
Argentina	63	55	51	11,256	84	541	44	49	2,217	57	75	22	27	67	58	26	43	32	93
Barbados	115	7	123	2,000	42	5,000	35	48	2,322	34	154	28	29	20	69	47	39	22	98
Bolivia	82	18	108	4,174	123	87	91	95	568	90	20	45	36	67	58	77	30	62	75
Brazil	90	14	86	6,004	107	198	59	55	1,792	66	64	59	44	84	54	49	38	36	92
Chile	43	88	52	11,247	68	1,263	47	52	1,904	61	70	54	43	9	72	41	40	36	92
Colombia	109	9	115	3,118	109	186	68	68	1,133	90	20	75	52	74	56	49	38	42	86
Costa Rica		—		—		—	52	58	1,616	50	92	62	46	83	55	54	37	32	93
Cuba	48	79	109	4,116	37	6,795	34	63	1,417	39	122	10	23	17	70	21	46	27	95
Dominican Rep.	82	18	92	5,263	59	2,053	70	76	958	84	24	93	73	60	59	36	41	67	68
Ecuador	77	24	90	5,606	80	652	64	67	1,143	76	43	65	47	51	60	59	35	57	79
El Salvador	102	10	79	6,857	54	2,286	82	82	744	84	24	107	89	94	50	66	32	72	63
Guatemala	96	12	101	4,722	76	780	86	75	1,002	94	19	112	96	115	33	86	27	84	50
Guyana	81	19	113	3,200	126	74	66	93	585	67	58	50	40	31	65	64	33	38	90
Haiti	128	3	121	2,285	81	576	122	127	198	130	4	124	124	118	32	73	31	113	26
Honduras	88	15	103	4,546	86	446	92	96	566	90	20	100	80	101	44	54	37	77	60
Jamaica	109	9	96	5,000	63	1,818	53	73	1,010	60	72	59	44	28	67	24	44	39	89
Mexico	102	10	82	6,330	95	321	58	56	1,779	56	80	62	46	23	68	82	28	55	81
Nicaragua	80	23	81	6,750	87	415	86	89	641	94	19	97	79	85	53	73	31	75	62
Panama	113	8	128	1,364	107	198	49	61	1,500	59	74	47	38	23	68	84	53	51	82
Paraguay	91	13	117	2,800	121	103	71	71	1,085	107	14	59	44	87	51	26	43	51	82
Peru	76	25	100	4,728	94	338	72	78	848	90	20	80	56	31	65	66	32	60	76
Trinidad & Tobago	91	13	39	15,000	49	2,941	43	35	3,868	33	155	75	52	67	58	57	36	36	92
Uruguay	56	59	85	6,179	72	982	45	46	2,386	74	48	36	33	60	59	17	47	30	94
Venezuela	68	42	37	16.595	77	764	47	42	2,952	36	135	54	43	71	57	41	40	51	82
EUROPE																			
NATO Europe		282		32,997		31,745			7,880		399		28		63		39		93
Belgium*	14	368	18	41,724	5	119,016	12	9	11,225	10	668	19	25	46	62	57	36	1	99
Denmark*	19	297	16	43,371	15	35,220	2	7	12,461	6	789	2	19	14	71	41	40	1	99
France*	10	424	13	44,525	12	41,431	3	11	10,749	12	560	10	23	23	68	59	35	1	99
Germany, West*	12	404	11	50,093	6	99,742	9	6	12,464	11	566	22	27	29	66	23	68	1	99
Greece	20	257	43	13,103	21	18,378	30	32	4,215	46	103	42	35	23	68	41	40	42	86
Iceland*		—		—		—	5	13	10,571	20	380	7	22	9	72	59	35	1	99
Italy*	29	136	32	21,266	19	25,770	21	26	5,677	25	259	10	23	51	60	36	41	27	95
Luxembourg*	34	117	17	42,000	23	16,154	13	5	13,746	5	827	15	24	46	62	82	28	1	99
Netherlands*	15	359	15	43,852	4	123,603	13	12	10,660	4	850	32	32	46	62	49	38	1	99
Norway*	16	357	21	37,282	43	4,485	3	10	10,919	3	857	3	20	17	70	49	38	1	99
Portugal	50	70	50	11,450	35	7,459	41	50	1,973	57	75	36	33	31	65	22	45	62	75
Turkey	59	57	104	4,516	48	3,274	75	64	1,387	74	48	87	62	98	46	92	25	75	62
United Kingdom*	17	342	7	59,306	8	78,508	16	23	7,214	21	360	7	22	4	79	59	35	1	99
ALL NATO (incl. US and Canada)		380		44,690		9,813			8,988		523		25		72		44		96
Warsaw Pact		342		26,755		5,449			4,133		191		29		61		49		99
Bulgaria*	39	106	83	6,267	31	8,476	32	39	3,678	37	134	32	32	74	56	6	50	30	94
Czechoslovakia*	28	148	49	11,598	22	17,592	25	29	5,213	32	161	42	35	60	59	36	41	1	99
Germany, East*	22	235	29	24,717	14	36,322	18	25	6,351	26	249	36	33	38	64	17	47	1	99
Hungary*	41	95	60	9,808	27	10,968	28	36	3,789	31	167	22	27	71	57	14	48	1	99
Poland*	35	111	45	12,264	26	12,472	29	37	3,785	41	112	47	38	51	60	6	50	1	99
Romania*	54	64	70	7,845	40	5,979	33	40	3,578	45	106	36	33	51	60	26	43	22	98
USSR*	9	433	25	31,165	41	5,089	23	34	4,052	29	210	27	28	49	61	6	50	1	99

	HEALTH										NUTRITION				WATER		
Public Expenditures per Capita		Population per Physician		Population per Hospital Bed		Infant Mortality Rate[5]		Life Expectancy[6]		Calorie Supply per Capita[7]		Calories as % of Requirements		% Population with Safe Water		
Rank	US$	Rank	Number	Rank	Number	Rank	Rate	Rank	Years	Rank	Number	Rank	%	Rank	%	
	85		1,182		268		95		61		2,607		107		56	**WORLD**
	320		430		100		20		72		3,440		134		94	Developed
	11		2,612		579		107		58		2,344		98		43	Developing
																AMERICA
	391		540		157		13		74		3,624		137		99	**North America**
12	383	20	540	34	164	13	13	7	74	3	3,652	7	138	5	99	United States*
9	460	23	550	23	112	10	12	7	74	23	3,358	28	126	5	99	Canada *
	23		1,413		338		72		64		2,449		103		55	**Latin America**
77	10	19	530	39	191	48	41	33	70	22	3,386	26	128	65	57	Argentina
40	72	51	1,390	28	125	38	27	33	70	35	3,054	28	126	1	100	Barbados
93	6	66	1,930	77	450	124	168	96	50	109	2,086	114	87	88	38	Bolivia
53	29	61	1,750	50	255	71	84	59	63	104	2,121	110	89	76	47	Brazil
49	42	57	1,640	56	277	47	40	49	67	52	2,732	57	112	33	87	Chile
68	15	65	1,910	90	596	67	77	64	62	76	2,364	75	102	59	62	Colombia
62	19	53	1,450	58	291	32	22	33	70	61	2,630	47	117	42	80	Costa Rica
47	45	35	730	45	223	28	19	19	72	53	2,717	42	118	13	98	Cuba
64	18	68	2,060	75	429	77	96	71	60	101	2,133	94	94	61	61	Dominican Republic
73	11	56	1,620	81	491	63	70	71	60	108	2,092	107	91	77	46	Ecuador
81	9	83	3,330	89	590	56	53	59	63	98	2,163	94	94	81	44	El Salvador
81	9	78	2,630	86	536	62	69	74	58	110	2,064	94	94	84	42	Guatemala
69	14	91	6,400	41	210	53	46	46	69	67	2,481	62	109	13	98	Guyana
121	2	94	7,090	129	1,421	98	130	95	51	125	1,882	124	83	121	10	Haiti
77	10	82	3,190	108	760	82	103	75	57	96	2,175	88	96	63	59	Honduras
52	32	80	2,940	55	271	24	16	33	70	64	2,570	50	115	39	82	Jamaica
70	13	60	1,740	115	844	63	70	55	65	50	2,803	39	120	67	55	Mexico
77	10	55	1,580	78	482	91	122	80	55	86	2,284	75	102	86	41	Nicaragua
41	70	48	1,150	52	264	55	47	33	70	83	2,289	84	99	39	82	Panama
95	5	63	1,830	107	740	58	58	57	64	43	2,902	28	126	110	17	Paraguay
84	8	54	1,470	87	545	75	92	75	57	97	2,166	102	92	70	53	Peru
36	84	52	1,440	46	225	35	24	33	70	56	2,702	57	112	29	89	Trinidad & Tobago
57	24	20	540	47	239	53	46	27	71	44	2,868	65	107	38	83	Uruguay
38	76	47	1,120	64	340	51	45	52	66	59	2,649	65	107	27	91	Venezuela
																EUROPE
	413		526		109		46		71		3,389		132		91	**NATO Europe**
10	454	5	410	22	109	10	12	19	72	6	3,583	9	136	29	89	Belgium*
2	823	16	480	27	120	5	9	7	74	14	3,495	24	130	5	99	Denmark*
6	654	28	580	8	82	8	10	11	73	21	3,390	15	134	18	97	France*
5	676	11	450	10	86	20	15	19	72	8	3,537	20	132	5	99	Germany, West*
30	122	7	420	33	159	28	19	11	73	19	3,400	9	136	18	97	Greece
8	602	11	450	1	59	9	11	1	76	37	3,013	56	113	5	99	Iceland*
21	262	2	350	19	98	20	15	11	73	4	3,650	3	145	35	86	Italy*
31	112	34	710	5	79	13	13	27	71	7	3,565	11	135	13	98	Luxembourg*
4	691	24	560	20	99	2	8	4	75	24	3,338	34	124	18	97	Netherlands*
3	721	18	520	3	66	5	9	4	75	27	3,288	35	123	13	98	Norway*
43	63	20	540	38	187	45	39	33	70	28	3,203	22	131	26	92	Portugal
73	11	58	1,710	83	503	93	125	68	61	38	2,965	42	118	50	69	Turkey
16	343	30	640	26	116	13	13	11	73	26	3,316	20	132	5	99	United Kingdom*
	404		533		126		32		72		3,491		134		94	**ALL NATO** (incl. US and Canada)
	104		317		86		32		70		3,480		135		64	**Warsaw Pact**
39	74	7	420	13	92	32	22	19	72	5	3,638	2	146		na	Bulgaria*
24	151	3	370	8	82	28	19	33	70	16	3,472	6	140	44	78	Czechoslovakia*
22	251	17	500	14	94	13	13	19	72	2	3,746	5	143	39	82	Germany, East *
32	110	5	410	25	114	35	24	33	70	9	3,533	15	134	81	44	Hungary*
27	127	27	570	29	131	32	22	27	71	11	3,520	15	134	67	55	Poland *
37	82	33	700	23	112	39	30	33	70	20	3,395	26	128		na	Romania*
34	91	1	270	6	80	42	36	46	69	17	3,460	11	135		na	USSR*

	MILITARY						GNP			EDUCATION									
	Public Expenditures per Capita		Public Expenditures per Soldier[1]		Public Expenditures per Sq. Km.		Economic-Social Standing[2]	per Capita		Public Expenditures per Capita		School-Age Population per Teacher[3]		% School-Age Population in School		% Women in Total University Enrollment		Literacy Rate[4]	
	Rank	US$	Rank	US$	Rank	US$	Avg. Rank	Rank	US$	Rank	US$	Rank	Number	Rank	Number	Rank	%	Rank	%
Other Europe		140		16,142		7,297			6,214		311		30		65		39		93
Albania	52	68	107	4,186	38	6,272	63	77	854	78	34	42	35	42	63	82	28	64	72
Austria*	35	111	33	22,000	30	9,976	18	17	9,058	15	511	15	24	74	56	49	38	1	99
Finland*	30	126	40	14,975	65	1,777	11	20	8,556	18	487	22	27	42	63	11	49	1	99
Ireland*	55	61	41	14,643	50	2,916	24	31	4,382	24	300	31	31	17	70	30	42	22	98
Malta	72	32	53	11,000	13	36,667	39	44	2,646	51	86	22	27	31	65	105	21	44	85
Spain	41	95	55	10.941	36	6,957	25	28	5,228	43	110	32	32	20	69	47	39	32	93
Sweden*	11	408	10	51,258	34	7,518	1	8	12,157	2	1,164	1	18	31	65	36	41	1	99
Switzerand*	18	324	3	108,210	11	49.782	10	4	15,623	6	789	46	37	42	63	73	31	1	99
Yugoslavia	40	97	66	8,293	32	8,397	38	47	2,365	39	122	36	33	51	60	41	40	44	85
ASIA																			
Middle East		298		26,510		6,041			2,308		117		50		51		30		46
Bahrain	13	381	5	70,500	3	235,000	46	27	5,492	30	186	65	47	94	50	5	52	96	40
Cyprus	61	56	112	3,500	45	3,804	37	43	2,870	47	97	32	32	60	59	36	41	44	85
Egypt[8]	66	46	101	4,722	61	1,862	90	102	462	94	19	88	64	98	46	73	31	84	50
Iran	33	119	31	22,445	52	2,723	69	51	1,946	42	111	75	52	74	56	66	32	89	49
Iraq	24	211	47	12,050	39	6,151	56	45	2,633	53	84	51	41	14	71	77	30	101	35
Israel*	3	1,464	24	33,374	2	266,346	22	30	4,917	19	389	3	20	31	65	24	44	40	88
Jordan	31	120	89	5,702	44	3,910	81	79	847	70	53	71	49	74	56	49	38	80	58
Kuwait	7	705	4	81,818	10	50,562	17	3	20,188	13	541	6	21	23	68	2	57	72	63
Lebanon	49	77	28	25,333	20	21,923	55		—		na	28	29	74	56	99	23	60	76
Oman	5	902	19	41,000	46	3,668	73	41	3,465	49	94	100	80	122	30		na	84	50
Qatar	1	4,762	2	200,000	7	90,909	31	1	22,428	1	2,667	3	20	14	71	1	58	122	20
Saudi Arabia	2	1,837	1	387,909	33	7,939	61	21	8,205	14	521	68	48	114	35	92	25	128	16
Syria	21	238	65	8,877	28	10,929	75	65	1,185	62	69	54	43	51	60	95	24	81	55
United Arab Emirates	4	1,321	12	46,040	24	13,768	36	2	21,796	28	226	21	26	87	51	30	42	121	21
Yemen, Arab Rep.	52	68	61	9,460	64	1,795	116	87	652	98	18	134	200	134	18	128	12	135	10
Yemen, People's Dem. Rep.	61	56	98	4,952	96	312	109	101	463	89	21	93	73	105	41	77	30	111	27
South Asia		6		2,991		1,014			193		6		84		38		27		38
Afghanistan	125	4	133	711	122	99	136	123	237	130	4	126	143	131	21	124	14	133	12
Bangladesh	133	1	126	1,697	74	896	133	138	109	135	2	120	115	118	32	111	19	107	29
India	117	6	111	3,531	69	1,117	115	128	197	121	6	97	79	107	40	86	27	96	40
Nepal	133	1	131	800	119	114	137	136	123	135	2	125	126	124	28	106	20	126	19
Pakistan	96	12	120	2,457	66	1,311	118	122	247	124	5	118	114	121	31	86	27	108	28
Sri Lanka	129	2	124	1,857	92	396	85	124	227	124	5	53	42	29	66	59	35	44	85
Far East		35		6,496		3,323			1,135		54		44		59		31		74
Brunei	6	808	8	57,333	17	29.655	27	15	10,357	27	230	7	22	7	74	6	50	71	64
Burma	117	6	129	1,112	102	279	113	133	152	135	2	121	121	105	41	11	49	65	70
Cambodia		na		—			126		—		na	105	86	125	27	111	19	90	48
China	72	32	77	7,339	47	3,334	83	100	474	105	16	51	41	51	60	77	30	65	70
Indonesia	96	12	78	7,159	75	844	108	113	319	121	6	79	53	85	53	91	26	69	65
Japan*	45	83	20	39,967	18	25.872	20	18	8,797	16	508	30	30	9	72	99	23	1	99
Korea, North	50	70	125	1,830	29	10,207	80	70	1,128	78	34	90	68	49	61	41	40	44	85
Korea, South	44	86	91	5,418	16	34,051	67	60	1,560	71	52	89	66	20	69	99	23	32	93
Laos	102	10	132	714	113	148	129	139	99		na	90	68	101	44	86	27	108	28
Malaysia	59	57	46	12,172	53	2,363	60	62	1,431	54	82	68	48	51	60	66	32	68	66
Mongolia	47	80	106	4,333	124	83	54	80	785	72	50	54	43	51	60	11	49	27	95
Philippines	91	13	84	6,223	58	2,137	78	90	624	111	12	80	56	74	56	3	55	41	87
Singapore	25	194	44	12,722	1	763,333	41	38	3,780	44	108	65	47	60	59	26	43	59	77
Taiwan	31	120	110	3,905	9	65,170	50	54	1,847	65	66	68	48	60	59	66	32	44	85
Thailand	77	24	94	5,213	56	2,191	86	94	573	98	18	54	43	94	50	30	42	50	84
Vietnam	86	17	130	880	51	2,730	102	132	162	121	6	71	49	42	63	66	32	56	80
OCEANIA		163		39,747		410			7,049		400		27		66		43		91
Australia*	23	213	14	43,886	90	400	6	19	8,699	17	505	10	23	9	72	22	45	1	99
Fiji	87	16	57	10,000	83	546	51	59	1,613	51	86	47	38	9	72	82	28	57	79
New Zealand*	35	111	27	26,615	67	1,288	15	24	6,716	23	336	15	24	2	84	30	42	1	99
Papua New Guinea	102	10	57	10,000	128	65	94	83	725	78	34	114	100	123	29	130	10	105	32

	HEALTH									NUTRITION			WATER		
	Public Expenditures per Capita		Population per Physician		Population per Hospital Bed		Infant Mortality Rate[5]		Life Expectancy[6]		Calorie Supply per Capita[7]		Calories as % of Requirements		% Population with Safe Water	
	Rank	US$	Rank	Number	Rank	Number	Rank	Rate	Rank	Years	Rank	Number	Rank	%	Rank	%
Other Europe		282		520		124		22		72		3,376		133		77
Albania	55	25	43	940	32	157	72	87	46	69	47	2,837	42	118		na
Austria *	11	453	7	420	12	88	20	15	19	72	14	3,495	18	133	31	88
Finland *	17	341	24	560	2	64	2	8	19	72	32	3,119	50	115	36	84
Ireland *	20	263	39	810	17	96	20	15	11	73	1	3,766	1	150	48	73
Malta	35	86	40	870	21	102	24	16	33	70	33	3,103	31	125	1	100
Spain	24	151	11	450	37	186	13	13	11	73	25	3,333	11	135	44	78
Sweden *	1	924	14	470	4	67	1	7	1	76	31	3,157	47	117	5	99
Switzerland *	7	625	10	430	11	87	5	9	4	75	10	3,525	22	131	23	96
Yugoslavia	27	127	37	740	35	168	40	32	33	70	12	3,511	7	138	64	58
ASIA																
Middle East		36		1,366		529		101		55		2,815		115		68
Bahrain	26	132	49	1,230	65	344	68	78	64	62		na		na	1	100
Cyprus	48	43	45	1,030	40	193	24	16	11	73	30	3,200	25	129	24	95
Egypt[8]	88	7	44	980	81	491	73	90	80	55	39	2,949	47	117	36	84
Iran	51	35	74	2,320	92	600	84	112	86	54	42	2,912	37	121	65	57
Iraq	61	21	67	1,980	84	505	75	92	80	55	60	2,643	60	110	50	69
Israel *	23	191	3	370	36	181	24	16	19	72	36	3,045	42	118	5	99
Jordan	62	19	73	2,280	126	1,195	78	97	78	56	74	2,397	87	97	56	66
Kuwait	19	289	30	640	51	257	45	39	33	70		na		na	44	78
Lebanon		na	28	580	49	247	51	45	55	65	66	2,496	78	101	27	91
Oman	44	60	59	1,730	93	605	110	142	106	47		na		na	104	22
Qatar		na	46	1,050	68	357	104	138	80	55		na		na	18	97
Saudi Arabia	29	123	62	1,790	105	724	88	118	96	50	62	2,624	63	108	57	64
Syria	95	5	75	2,360	119	941	69	81	64	62	45	2,863	50	115	50	69
United Arab Emirates	18	327	40	870	125	1,129	59	65	86	54		na		na	31	88
Yemen, Arab Rep.	93	6	104	9,990	134	1,790	126	170	132	42	87	2,272	94	94	128	4
Yemen, People's Dem. Rep.	105	4	103	9,310	103	710	120	160	122	44	120	1,945	125	81	89	37
South Asia		2		4,180		1,385		135		51		2,014		90		41
Afghanistan	127	1	120	15,910	139	4,662	134	185	132	42	129	1,833	131	75	121	10
Bangladesh	105	4	107	10,890	138	4,313	106	139	106	47	126	1,877	119	85	54	68
India	121	2	85	3,760	128	1,287	102	134	91	52	117	1,998	108	90	86	41
Nepal	127	1	132	36,520	140	5,874	100	133	127	43	122	1,914	114	87	121	10
Pakistan	127	1	86	3,820	131	1,651	110	142	91	52	81	2,300	81	100	94	29
Sri Lanka	95	5	92	6,640	66	346	50	42	52	66	90	2,249	78	101	105	21
Far East		34		2,377		411		67		63		2,474		107		46
Brunei		na	72	2,130	61	326	31	20	52	66		na		na	49	72
Burma	127	1	88	4,800	124	1,124	107	140	89	53	84	2,286	70	106	100	23
Cambodia		na	140	57,670	120	951	117	150	121	45	131	1,795	125	81	79	45
China	88	7	77	2,530	85	524	57	56	57	64	69	2,472	73	105		na
Indonesia	105	4	110	11,940	133	1,782	74	91	96	50	82	2,295	70	106	106	19
Japan *	13	378	38	780	14	94	2	8	1	76	41	2,916	31	125	13	98
Korea, North	112	3	76	2,500	117	891	63	70	59	63	47	2,837	37	121		na
Korea, South	112	3	64	1,860	101	663	43	37	59	63	40	2,946	31	125	43	79
Laos	127	1	123	17,200	121	1,022	128	175	132	42	128	1,856	122	84	75	48
Malaysia	58	22	97	7,600	60	324	44	38	49	67	58	2,650	42	118	57	64
Mongolia	73	11	15	460	14	94	63	70	59	63	54	2,711	57	112		na
Philippines	112	3	79	2,860	94	611	59	65	68	61	78	2,315	75	102	67	55
Singapore	45	56	50	1,240	48	244	13	13	27	71	34	3,100	11	135	1	100
Taiwan	46	48	42	900		na	37	25	27	71		na		na		na
Thailand	105	4	96	7,300	113	834	61	68	68	61	80	2,301	74	104	100	23
Vietnam	127	1	89	5,700	54	265	86	115	64	62	113	2,029	94	94	98	24
OCEANIA		296		680		94		43		70		3,111		117		84
Australia *	15	350	24	560	6	80	10	12	7	74	29	3,202	39	120	18	97
Fiji	50	36	71	2,100	70	379	48	41	27	71		na		na	50	69
New Zealand *	14	372	32	670	18	97	19	14	11	73	12	3,511	18	133	25	93
Papua New Guinea	64	18	119	15,330	52	264	83	106	96	50	84	2,286	117	86	114	16

141 Countries, 1979   **TABLE III**

	MILITARY						GNP		EDUCATION									
	Public Expenditures per Capita		Public Expenditures per Soldier [1]		Public Expenditures per Sq. Km.		Economic-Social Standing [2]	per Capita		Public Expenditures per Capita		School-Age Population per Teacher [3]		% School-Age Population in School		% Women in Total University Enrollment		Literacy Rate [4]	
	Rank	US$	Rank	US$	Rank	US$	Avg. Rank	Rank	US$	Rank	US$	Rank	Number	Rank	Number	Rank	%	Rank	%
AFRICA		24		8,719		349			723		33		90		41		22		32
Algeria	71	33	80	6,764	104	253	74	57	1,710	38	131	85	59	74	56	95	24	100	37
Angola		—		—		—	99	84	723	102	17	86	61	94	50	30	42	129	15
Benin	122	5	67	8,000	114	142	120	116	282	107	14	129	158	115	33	113	18	120	22
Botswana	69	35	26	27,000	130	45	84	86	690	67	58	75	52	74	56	54	37	101	35
Burundi	117	6	96	5,000	73	899	135	131	190	124	5	138	295	139	11	116	17	119	23
Cameroon	102	10	53	11,000	110	185	104	91	608	94	19	111	91	87	51	122	15	94	42
Central African Rep.	117	6	42	14,000	133	22	125	118	271	111	12	127	155	111	36	134	8	113	26
Chad	109	9	67	8,000	131	31	140	136	123	132	3	139	319	137	17	136	5	127	18
Congo	70	34	75	7,429	111	152	89	85	698	69	56	73	50	5	75	126	13	81	55
Equatorial Guinea	77	24	87	6,000	106	214	106	92	602		na	103	84	67	58		na	122	20
Ethiopia	96	12	127	1,572	99	286	141	135	131	132	3	137	294	134	18	120	16	140	7
Gabon	38	108	23	34,500	103	258	56	33	4,060	35	151	62	46	1	90	95	24	96	40
Gambia		—		—		—	131	126	215	106	15	116	107	131	21		—	133	12
Ghana	122	5	116	3,000	105	252	110	107	381	111	12	80	56	104	43	126	13	101	35
Guinea		—		—		—	131	117	274	111	12	132	188	134	18	130	10	129	15
Ivory Coast	91	13	35	19.600	97	304	93	69	1,132	47	97	107	89	109	38	106	20	116	25
Kenya	82	18	30	24,250	85	499	97	108	373	87	23	84	58	31	65	106	20	91	45
Lesotho		—		—		—	98	109	359	118	8	95	75	71	57	17	47	77	60
Liberia	115	7	119	2,600	117	117	107	99	511	82	29	105	86	109	38	103	22	122	20
Libya	27	171	48	11,905	100	284	39	22	7,962	22	358	19	25	7	74	103	22	94	42
Madagascar	102	10	74	7,454	116	140	103	111	331	102	17	113	97	87	51	77	30	84	50
Malawi	113	8	62	9,400	91	397	127	125	218	124	5	131	186	111	36	124	14	111	27
Mali	117	6	63	9,250	132	30	138	129	196	118	8	135	238	138	16	130	10	135	10
Mauritania	65	47	71	7,778	127	68	127	111	331	102	17	136	274	133	19		na	129	15
Mauritius	129	2		na	71	1,000	62	72	1,083	63	68	36	33	38	64	113	18	51	82
Morocco	67	44	64	9,143	60	2,006	95	81	760	73	49	107	89	111	36	92	25	117	24
Mozambique	102	10	99	4,750	114	142	121	114	315	132	3	133	190	101	44	64	33	117	24
Niger	129	2	87	6,000	134	9	134	115	289	111	12	140	337	139	11	116	17	139	8
Nigeria	74	27	56	10,316	57	2,155	101	73	1,010	78	34	103	84	107	40	122	15	108	28
Rwanda	56	59	105	4,500	78	684	130	130	194	124	5	130	185	115	33	133	9	106	30
Senegal	125	4	76	7,375	98	301	118	104	456	98	18	127	155	129	23	106	20	135	10
Sierra Leone	100	11	117	2,667	120	112	124	120	261	116	11	117	108	127	26	120	16	129	15
Somalia	129	2	122	2,065	112	149	123	106	389	120	7	122	122	129	23	129	11	141	5
South Africa	74	27	22	36,016	62	1,858	65	53	1,882	55	81	83	57	60	59	95	24	69	65
Sudan	46	81	114	3,159	125	79	117	110	337	98	18	118	114	125	27	99	23	122	20
Swaziland	100	11	57	10,000	82	575	78	87	652	77	39	73	50	38	64	6	50	91	45
Tanzania	82	18	95	5,135	101	282	112	121	253	107	14	102	81	87	51	134	8	77	60
Togo	88	15	72	7,667	89	405	105	105	390	84	24	97	79	38	64	116	17	113	26
Tunisia	109	9	38	16,500	55	2,219	77	66	1,146	64	67	90	68	87	51	66	32	91	45
Uganda	58	58	72	7,667	79	682	111	103	461	117	9	122	122	127	26	113	18	101	35
Upper Volta	91	13	67	8,000	117	117	139	133	152	124	5	141	608	141	8	106	20	138	9
Zaire	122	5	93	5,238	129	47	114	119	266	110	13	96	78	98	46	136	5	96	40
Zambia	125	4	34	21,000	93	391	96	97	546	83	26	107	89	87	51	116	17	81	55
Zimbabwe	64	52	36	19,409	70	1,093	99	98	524	88	22	115	106	118	32	86	27	84	50

* Developed country
— none or negligible   na Not available
1. ''Soldier'' represents all members of the armed forces.
2. Represents average of ranks for GNP per capita, education, and health. See notes, page 37.
3. Ages 5-19.
4. Represents % of adult population (over 15) able to read and write.
5. Deaths under one year per 1,000 live births.
6. Expectation of life at birth.
7. Per capita supply of food, including fish, in calories.
8. Egypt is shown in the political grouping of Middle East states rather than in Africa.

RANK shows the standing of the country among those in the table. The rank order number is repeated if more than one country has the same figure.

Public Expenditures per Capita		Population per Physician		Population per Hospital Bed		Infant Mortality Rate[5]		Life Expectancy[6]		Calorie Supply per Capita[7]		Calories as % of Requirements		% Population with Safe Water		
Rank	US$	Rank	Number	Rank	Number	Rank	Rate	Rank	Years	Rank	Number	Rank	%	Rank	%	
	7		8,260		536		146		48		2,243		96		32	**AFRICA**
58	22	84	3,630	71	389	95	127	78	56	73	2,406	81	100	44	78	Algeria
88	7	121	16,360	62	327	137	192	139	41	105	2,110	108	90	110	17	Angola
105	4	122	16,560	100	662	116	149	108	46	79	2,310	81	100	110	17	Benin
67	16	98	7,640	63	330	78	97	96	50	95	2,181	94	94	79	45	Botswana
121	2	136	41,920	116	850	107	140	127	43	100	2,152	102	92		na	Burundi
95	5	114	13,800	69	371	118	157	122	44	70	2,451	70	106	73	49	Cameroon
105	4	130	27,190	96	631	136	190	122	44	99	2,161	88	96	108	18	Central African Rep.
127	1	138	50,310	127	1,217	122	165	127	43	130	1,808	130	76	96	26	Chad
58	22	90	5,030	44	213	132	180	108	46	94	2,200	84	99	117	13	Congo
	na	135	40,670	73	404	122	165	108	46		na		na		na	Equatorial Guinea
121	2	141	59,950	137	3,146	130	178	141	40	132	1,729	132	74	117	13	Ethiopia
42	64	81	3,180	30	136	130	178	127	43	46	2,844	36	122	129	1	Gabon
84	8	110	11,940	112	814	140	217	139	41	89	2,250	94	94	120	12	Gambia
105	4	100	7,920	102	687	86	115	102	48	116	2,016	112	88	72	50	Ghana
112	3	124	17,580	97	634	141	220	122	44	121	1,934	122	84	121	10	Guinea
64	18	118	15,520	110	809	104	138	108	46	63	2,623	55	114	106	19	Ivory Coast
88	7	106	10,520	95	613	70	83	89	53	111	2,055	112	88	98	24	Kenya
95	5	112	13,050	80	487	85	114	96	50	71	2,442	65	107	100	23	Lesotho
73	11	102	9,190	104	717	114	148	102	48	68	2,474	65	107	121	10	Liberia
33	105	35	730	41	210	98	130	80	55	18	3,418	3	145	33	87	Libya
88	7	105	10,180	74	408	81	102	108	46	72	2,436	65	107	96	26	Madagascar
121	2	137	48,850	90	596	110	142	108	46	91	2,219	88	96	81	44	Malawi
121	2	128	21,550	135	1,791	139	210	132	42	118	1,996	119	85	100	23	Mali
95	5	117	14,740	136	2,653	135	187	132	42	112	2,051	110	89	110	17	Mauritania
53	29	70	2,090	59	293	41	34	49	67	55	2,703	41	119	62	60	Mauritius
84	8	108	11,310	111	812	100	133	80	55	57	2,651	60	110	70	53	Morocco
	na	133	37,000	109	781	114	148	108	46	124	1,891	125	81	127	7	Mozambique
112	3	134	38,190	130	1,641	138	200	132	42	92	2,217	94	94	73	49	Niger
95	5	109	11,330	123	1,069	118	157	102	48	77	2,335	84	99	95	28	Nigeria
127	1	131	30,970	99	646	95	127	108	46	93	2,202	92	95	54	68	Rwanda
95	5	115	13,830	118	900	120	160	122	44	88	2,261	92	95	91	35	Senegal
112	3	125	17,890	114	840	103	136	108	46	106	2,106	102	92	126	8	Sierra Leone
112	3	113	13,360	88	559	129	177	127	43	103	2,131	102	92	93	30	Somalia
84	8	68	2,060	31	155	78	97	71	60	49	2,827	50	115		na	South Africa
112	3	101	8,390	122	1,031	109	141	108	46	75	2,371	78	101	77	46	Sudan
70	13	93	6,760	57	289	125	168	108	46	65	2 499	63	108	89	37	Swaziland
95	5	126	18,080	79	484	93	125	91	52	114	2,025	114	87	92	33	Tanzania
81	9	127	18,300	106	738	90	121	108	46	106	2,106	102	92	117	13	Togo
55	25	87	4,210	76	442	92	123	75	57	51	2,751	50	115	59	62	Tunisia
95	5	129	24,840	98	636	89	120	91	52	127	1,862	128	80	114	16	Uganda
127	1	139	55,510	132	1.755	133	182	132	42	115	2,018	119	85	116	14	Upper Volta
112	3	116	14,700	67	354	127	171	108	46	101	2,133	88	96	108	18	Zaire
72	12	99	7,910	43	212	113	144	102	48	119	1,992	117	86	84	42	Zambia
77	10	95	7,140	72	390	97	129	86	54	123	1,911	128	80		na	Zimbabwe

NOTES ON DATA

The notes following provide a brief background on definitions and sources, and are intended to alert the general reader to some of the measurement problems in an international compilation of this kind. Readers wishing to use the detailed figures for analytical purposes are urged to consult the original sources, which more adequately convey the scope and qualifications of the data.

Specific queries may be addressed to the author (Box 1003, Leesburg, Virginia 22075). Professional comments and suggestions are welcome at all times, and particularly from national statistical services which could add to the accuracy of the reporting.

Revisions In compiling this eighth edition of *World Military and Social Expenditures*, all statistics were reviewed and corrected to include the most recent data available for the 141 countries that are covered. Because of revisions by original sources and the changes in sources that are sometimes necessary, the detailed national data in Table III cannot be used as a time series, or to judge trends.

Time frame Although the statistical tables were largely prepared in 1982, the latest year for which adequate world-wide coverage was possible for many of the social statistics was 1979, and for some it was 1978. Social data tend to lag behind military. Projections to 1979 were therefore necessary for some of the social statistics, while military, population, and GNP data were generally available through 1980.

Qualifications of the data In the post-war period there has been a major leap forward in the availability and reliability of data for international comparisons. Nevertheless, any world compendium of this sort inevitably represents subjective judgments in selecting and presenting statistics, and includes data that are uneven in quality. Numerous factors affect comparability and suggest caution in making comparisons between countries. For example:

1. Some statistical systems, especially in developing nations, are in the early stages of development; beyond urban areas, coverage may be nonexistent or extremely sparse.

2. The practice of limited disclosure of statistics continues particularly in countries under communist governments. In these cases the range of error in estimates made by foreign experts is unknown and may be wide. Most of the figures shown for Albania, China, Cuba, Laos, Mongolia, North Korea, Vietnam, and the Warsaw Pact countries are subject to considerable uncertainty and must be regarded as very rough approximations.

3. Hostilities in Cambodia and Lebanon have restricted the flow of information from those countries. Where estimates are shown, they are rough benchmark data, largely based on earlier years.

4. Variations in definitions and concepts may significantly affect comparability. These occur even under the most advanced reporting systems.

5. Per capita figures based on national totals reveal nothing of the pattern of distribution in incomes and welfare within countries. Differences within nations in those patterns may mean significant differences in the level of living of the average citizen which are not apparent in gross indicators.

Gross National Product

Gross National Product is the economy's total output of goods and services, valued at current market prices paid by the ultimate consumer.

GNP, as stated above, is the most comprehensive measure of the national economy, but it does not cover some important areas of economic activity. Household services and that part of the product which is outside the market are not included in the GNP. For this reason, it is likely to be more representative, as a measure of overall product, for developed economies than for developing. The difference in coverage does not invalidate comparisons between the two groups of countries, but it may tend to exaggerate the contrast between them.

The GNP figures are drawn from the data fund of the World Bank. For this report, the Bank's calculations in national currencies are converted to dollars using single-year exchange rates.

Military

National military expenditures are current and capital expenditures to meet the needs of the armed forces. They include military assistance to foreign countries and the military components of nuclear, space, and research and development programs.

By custom and accounting practice, national military budgets usually do not include expenditures for veterans' benefits, interest on war debts, civil defense, and outlays for strategic industrial stockpiling. Military budgets also may exclude all or part of national intelligence expenditures. Adding these items to regular defense budgets would greatly enlarge the total of annual public expenditures which are military-related, but adequate information to determine precisely how such costs affect various national expenditures and their overall size world-wide is not available at present. There are also substantial social costs which are extra-budgetary, including manpower underpriced because of conscription, and the tax exemptions accorded military properties. Because costs such as these are not reflected in official budgets, military expenditures tend to understate the burden on the economy.

A standard definition of military expenditures, as paraphrased above, is used by the members of NATO and, in so far as it is possible to do so, it is the concept followed in this report, but major differences in national accounting systems make it impossible to achieve general uniformity.

In Warsaw Pact and other communist countries, the scope of the accounting for military programs is not clear and data are necessary highly speculative. Some of the uncertainties and problems in preparing estimates are discussed on pages 38-39.

Armed forces represent manpower in the regular forces, including conscripts. Paramilitary forces and reservists are not included.

The manpower figures in the tables cover regular forces only, on the premise that these provide the most consistent basis for international comparison, and also are covered by military budgets. Paramilitary forces (armed border guards and gendarmerie) vary considerably in their potential for prompt and efficient military action, as do reservists, who serve for a short period in the year. (The addition of paramilitary and reservist forces would triple the world total of men under arms.)

In individual countries, the significance of the size of the force will depend on their equipment, training, technical proficiency, and morale, and also (as in the US) on the use made of civilians in functions that are performed by the military in other countries. Some countries have universal, automatic draft for relatively short periods; others, like the US, depend on volunteers, who serve on a career basis and generally for longer periods of time.

IISS, the recognized international authority on force levels, also publishes data on paramilitary forces, people's militia, and reservists.

Arms trade represents the movement through official channels of conventional military equipment and of commodities considered primarily military in nature. Nuclear materials are excluded.

The export-import estimates in Table I and *charts 1 and 3* are compiled by ACDA, and generally conform to the definition above. The data include weapons, military aircraft and ships, ammunition, and uniforms, and exclude foodstuffs, medical equipment, and other items with alternative civilian uses. They are trade figures, and therefore do not include orders or agreements which may result in future transfers, nor do they cover training or services associated with the equipment transfers. They also omit other significant routes for arms shipments (see page 9).

Military trainees are foreign forces trained in a sponsoring country, or trained at home courtesy of foreign military technicians.

The US data, reported annually by DOD, refer to training in the US only; larger numbers are trained abroad. UK information is from a Parliamentary response, reported in Hansard April 1982, and refers to countries whose nationals received training on UK military training courses. Information on military training by the USSR, which was included in *WMSE 82*, is no longer published by CIA.

Military Bases and Forces Abroad

Information on overseas installations and forces is scattered and incomplete. For USSR, Cuba, and E. Germany, the available data may also overstate the totals since, in the absence of consistent alternative sources, the numbers shown have been taken from the US DOD publication, *Soviet Military Power*, and include civilian as well as military personnel.

Other sources used for *map 1* and the table were: IISS Adelphi Paper 176 (for official NATO estimates of Soviet forces in Central Europe), IISS *Military Balance, The Economist*, 1981 British White Paper, and *Jeune Afrique*. Data on US installations and forces, are from annual DOD reports submitted to the US Congress.

Wars and Deaths

Wars and estimated deaths in *map 3* are from records maintained by William Eckhardt, Director, Peace Research Laboratory, St. Louis, Missouri. His principal sources are: Azar's conflict and peace data bank of the University of Maryland, lists of wars published by Bouthoul & Carrère in *Peace Research*, and battle deaths in Singer and Small's computer records at the University of Michigan. These records were supplemented by news sources available through July 1982.

Information on deaths associated with wars is incomplete, and Eckhardt emphasizes that all estimates must be used with caution. No central official records are kept. Civilian deaths are less reliable than battle deaths and are often unavailable. War-related famine was a major cause of high death rates in conflicts in Nigeria, Bangladesh, and Cambodia.

Military Control and Repression

In establishing the list of military-dominated governments for *map 4*, the following criteria were considered: existence of a state of martial law; key political leadership by military officers; regimes recently established by military coups; a legal system based on military courts; links between military forces and political police.

The principal sources of information were: *The Statesman's Yearbook, The People's Almanac, Deadline Data on World Affairs, Political Handbook of the World*, and *The World Factbook*.

Governments are classified as "highly repressive" or "repressive" if they show a consistent pattern of violation of those human rights relating to personal safety. The most extreme uses of force against citizens—torture, brutality, and other forms of physical abuse—are usually associated with official violence on a broad scale and are considered "highly repressive". Other deprivations of civil liberties, such as arbitrary arrest and imprisonment, denial of public trial, invasion of the home, are classified as "repressive".

The principal sources of information consulted were: *Amnesty International Annual Reports* and AI files; *Freedom at Issue;* US Department of State *Country Reports on Human Rights Practices*, Council of Hemispheric Affairs *Human Rights in Latin America*, and Human Rights Internet files.

Since the political role of the military and governments' violation of human rights vary both in degree and in the evidence available, classifying a country as "military-dominated" and as "repressive" was necessarily a matter of subjective judgment in a number of cases, and may well be open to dispute.

Nuclear Weapons

Nuclear reactors—The world's inventory of nuclear reactors, shown in *chart 4*, and on the map, pages 12-13, are from *Nuclear News, Nuclear Engineering International*, the International Atomic Energy Agency and, for the US, the US Department of Energy. Power reactors are as of December 31, 1981; research reactors, reported by IAEA May 1980, represent responses to a questionnaire sent out in 1978.

Nuclear tests—Nuclear explosions, as shown on *chart 5*, are from the *SIPRI Yearbook 1982*.

Nuclear weapons—Although generally described as strategic or tactical, the distinction between these two categories of nuclear weapons is basically artificial, and subject to various interpretations. In this report we have tended to follow prevailing US concepts. All figures are approximate, and in this period of force modernization they are changing rapidly.

Charts 6 and 14 and *map 2* count as strategic those nuclear weapons that are intercontinental in range. For US and USSR they are weapons on intercontinental carriers: bombers, missiles, and submarines. For UK and France, they are weapons in submarines only, and for China, they are a rough guess of available ICBM's. The latter three countries also have weapons of continental range, i.e., able to reach the homeland of the adversary (presumably the USSR in this case); under the US concept, these are counted as "tactical".

Map 2 updates the inventory of nuclear power reactors through December 1981. It also extends the coverage of weapons locations, drawing on: the nuclear weapons research project of the Institute for Policy Studies (especially for eastern and southern Europe); the *Stern* report on nuclear weapons in West Germany; and the *Military Posture for FY 1983* of the US Joint Chiefs of Staff, for major air bases and ICBM sites in China.

Education

Public education expenditures represent current and capital expenditures by governments for public education and subsidized private education for pre-school through university levels.

In compiling information on public education expenditures, UNESCO attempts to cover such expenditures at local and intermediate levels of government as well as central government. Despite steady progress in data collection, the coverage is more complete at the central level than at lower levels.

Where necessary, UNESCO data for 1979 were supplemented by information from national statistical journals, or from national accounts compiled by OECD, UN, and IMF.

Since private education expenditures are not covered here, and nations vary greatly in the ratio of private to public spending, comparisons of total national expenditures may differ significantly from those for public only. In the US, for example, private funds cover about 19 percent of all education expenditures. In centrally planned economies, non-public funding is also significant, although it is likely to be a smaller proportion of the total.

Teachers and students are those in both public and private schools, through secondary or high school levels, not including pre-school, vocational, and adult education.

The count of teachers generally covers full-time and the full-time equivalent of part-time classroom teachers. It does not include supervisors or librarians. Reports now available from China on the number of teachers have revised upward sharply the estimates previously used for that country.

Women in university enrollment represent the percent of women in the total enrollment of universities and equivalent degree-granting institutions.

As a general rule, these figures exclude enrollment in teacher training at the third level and in technical colleges.

Literacy rates represent the proportion of the adult population (generally 15 years and over) able to both read and write.

Standardized tests for literacy generally focus on basic skills, the ability to read and write on a lower elementary school level. The concept of literacy is changing, however, particularly in industrialized countries, where there is increased awareness of the requirement for functional literacy, sometimes defined as the ability to read instructions necessary for a job or a license. By these standards, illiteracy is much more common than present rates suggest.

Health Care

Public health expenditures represent current and capital expenditures by governments for medical care and other health services.

They include national health insurance, public health, health expenditures under workmen's compensation, and in some countries, public expenditures for family planning, social welfare and social security. They do not include private health expenditures (and it should be noted that the ratio of private to public spending varies greatly among nations).

Like education expenditures, health expenditures by governments are understated for some countries and in the world total because of incomplete reporting at intermediate and local levels of government. To the extent that they include outlays for health care for military personnel, however, they overstate the size of civilian programs and represent some double counting.

In addition to variations in coverage, WHO cautions that differences in budgetary concepts and definitions of health seriously qualify comparisons among countries. While world and regional totals are believed to be reasonably representative, national data if used for comparisons should be studied in conjunction with other measures of national health care.

Physicians refer to fully qualified doctors practicing in the country.

This is intended to be a count of doctors in actual practice, teaching, or performing research within the country. National reporting, however, may reflect differences in definition, as well as in qualifications and training of physicians. Some countries include registered physicians who are inactive or who are practising elsewhere. Some, including Italy and USSR, count dentists as physicians. Some report only physicians in government service. Despite these shortcomings, the national data on physicians are probably more reliable for inter-country comparisons than are expenditure figures.

A sharply revised total number of physicians in China, reflecting reports received by WHO, significantly raised the physician count for developing nations as a whole in 1976. China has stressed the training of "barefoot doctors", and their wide dispersion through the countryside.

Infant mortality rates are the death rates of infants under 1 year of age per 1,000 live births.

In developing countries where registration systems are not fully effective, the rate is likely to understate infant deaths. Regional and other averages are derived from birth and death statistics.

Life expectancy is the average number of years of life expected at birth.

Rates reflect infant mortality as well as the life span thereafter.

Water

Two sets of data provide a rough indication of the proportion of the population served by an adequate system of water supply. It was necessary to combine information available from two sources to give world coverage to the important factor of water supply.

For developed nations, and for European nations classed as developing, the data show the percent of dwellings with piped water, based on the latest available information provided by national governments to the UN housing survey.

For most developing nations, the standard of adequacy is different, and somewhat lower. The data for these countries show the percent of the population with reasonable access to a "safe water supply", as reported to WHO. Safe means treated or uncontaminated water. Reasonable access in urban areas may include a public fountain if located not more than 200 meters from a house; in rural areas it means that the source of water is close enough not to require a disproportionate part of the day to fetch it. The information in most cases relates to 1980; for the remaining countries it is for 1975 or an earlier year in the 1970's.

Nutrition

Calories and protein per capita represent the average daily food supply available at the retail level after allowance for animal feed, seed, storage and marketing losses, and waste.

Dietary energy supplies are national averages for 1978-1980, as reported by FAO. Maldistribution of food within countries may mean that individual diets vary significantly from these averages. Caloric requirements are FAO estimates as of January 1980 of intake required to maintain moderate activity, taking account of the age/sex structure of the population, climate, etc.

Foreign Economic Aid

Foreign economic aid is net official economic aid distributed to less developed countries and multilateral agencies with the promotion of economic development as its chief objective.

Military supporting assistance is excluded from these figures insofar as it is possible to do so. There is, however, a gray area of quasi-military transactions which may appear in some national totals.

National figures include credits of a concessional character as well as grants. Amounts shown are after repayments and interest. Estimates for communist countries are approximations. Aid is reported by OECD in dollars at official rates of exchange.

International Peacekeeping

International peacekeeping expenditures represent official contributions in cash or in kind to support major peacekeeping forces and peace observation missions.

The UN-supported peacekeeping operations for which contributions were recorded in 1979 included UN Emergency Forces, Operation des Nations-Unies au Congo, UN Force in Cyprus, UN Truce Supervision Organization, UN Military Observer Group in India and Pakistan, and UN Interim Force in Lebanon.

The national amounts shown in the tables include, in addition to contributions in cash, rough estimates of costs of contributed airlifts, troops, and supplies, for which countries did not claim reimbursement. For those operations which were financed out of the UN regular budget, estimates of national expenditures were based on an allotment of the overall costs to individual countries according to UN assessment rates.

Exchange Rates

In making international comparisons of value data, the choice of conversion rates so radically affects results that a statement on this point is owed the reader. There is at present no wholly adequate basis for converting national currencies into a common denominator such as US dollars. To compare GNP and public expenditures between countries, the conversion rates should, ideally, reflect the internal purchasing power of each currency for the particular mix of goods and services in its economy.

Although statistical work on such parity rates is underway, under international sponsorship, the availability of purchasing power parities for a large selection of countries is some distance in the future.

Like other compilations of international statistics, this report in most instances uses annual average exchange rates for conversion from national currencies to dollars. These rates measure currency relations in internationally-traded goods. They are by no means ideal for conversion of GNP and national budgets but they do provide a rough basis for inter-country comparisons. Since they are in general use for this report we are also now applying them (modified by recent inflation in the US) to the European centrally-planned countries.

Official exchange rates are often subject to abrupt changes. As a result of these up and down shifts, a nation can seem to have moved into affluence, or depression, from one year to the next. In an effort to reduce the effect of such distortions, the World Bank in most cases uses a weighted average exchange rate for a three-year period for its calculations of national GNP in dollar equivalents. The choice of a single rather than multiple year exchange rate in this report was dictated largely by a need for comparability with other data which are reported by the original sources in current dollars on the basis of prevailing exchange rates.

Price Deflators

International comparisons with earlier years are affected by internal price trends as well as by changes in parities. To eliminate the impact of these fluctuations in the historical series, both military expenditures and GNP have been adjusted to the price base and exchange rates of 1979. The GNP deflators developed by the World Bank have been used for the price correction of both GNP and military expenditures. The two series in constant as well as current dollars appear in Table I, page 26.

Economic-Social Rank

Table III includes a single figure for each nation to summarize its rank among all nations in economic-social indicators. Three factors are combined: GNP per capita, education, and health. The method of averaging gives equal importance to each of the three elements. For education and health, this means that a summary rank is first obtained for the five indicators shown under each category.

The ranking method makes it possible to combine a variety of indicators. Other combinations are, of course, possible, and will be further explored. In this case, the indicators chosen for education and health represent both input of national effort (e.g. public expenditures, teachers) and output (e.g. literacy, infant mortality). Input factors give credit for effort, which will determine social progress but may not yet show in slower-acting indicators of results.

There are obvious omissions in coverage at present. Housing is one and nutrition is covered only through mortality and life expectancy. Perhaps even more important, only one of the eleven indicators now in the composite (% women in total university enrollment) begins to reflect the unequal distribution of resources within countries. One objective for future editions is to incorporate available data on distribution of incomes into the averages. □

Estimating Military Expenditures of the USSR and its Warsaw Pact Allies

In the absence of adequate reporting by the Soviet Union of its annual military expenditures, independent calculations must be made by western authorities (table opposite). A review of the estimates made by official US sources indicates that they tend to exaggerate Soviet military expenditures. The result is a stimulus to the arms race.

If the Soviet Union has an interest in curbing the momentum of the arms competition, it could take a relatively simple step: make public its military budget in the detail proposed by the United Nations for all countries. At a small sacrifice of secrecy, it could thereby provide the kind of reassurance on which mutual trust between nations and arms restraint depend.

The usual statistical note on Soviet military expenditures was expanded in *WMSE 1980* to give an overview of the range of western estimates and a more detailed evaluation of the official US estimates. The summary is repeated in this edition, with some revisions based on CIA testimony made available in the past year. Given the limitations of space and time, this is necessarily a cursory examination of a very complex subject. Hopefully it will provide some encouragement to others to explore further.[1]

Soviet military expenditures warrant special attention for several reasons:

1. As a summary of the Soviet military effort and trend, they affect US and all NATO planning, the willingness of public officials to spend more to meet the competition, and of taxpayers to bear the burden.
2. Unlike other major industrial powers, the Soviet Union fails to provide detail on its military budget, or even to describe what expenditures are covered. It announces a single undefined figure each year, which seldom changes. Since 1970 the budget has dropped about 4 percent, from 17.9 to 17.2 billion rubles.
3. The Soviet announced budget is clearly incomplete in view of the advanced military technology and the size of the military force the USSR has produced.
4. The ruble is almost exclusively a domestic currency and official rates of exchange reflect neither the relation between internal prices and foreign prices, nor balance of payments forces.
5. Between the official Soviet military budget, converted to dollars at the official rate, and the official US view of that budget, there was a gap of 155 billion dollars in 1979, a disparity which was larger than the total US military budget that year.
6. Between the official US estimate of Soviet military expenditures, and the estimate in this study, the gap was $67 billion in 1979, although we continue to use the CIA ruble estimate for the calculation.

In the discussion following, the principal focus is on the calculations by US intelligence agencies which establish the official US view of Soviet military expenditures. Since this publication also has dollar estimates for other Warsaw Pact countries lower than the US official estimates, the basis for the alternatives will be described as well.

Soviet expenditures in rubles

Basis of estimates

In the absence of adequate reporting by the Soviet Union, western analysts have generally resorted to one of two basic approaches to an estimate of Soviet military expenditures in rubles.

Add-on—One approach attempts to flesh out the Soviet announced military budget by adding elements such as research and development, which are believed to be missing from the official figures. The missing elements are generally extracted from other parts of the state budget.

Building-block—The other approach is independent of the Soviet announced budgets except in the valuation of research expenditures. This method breaks down military expenditures into physical quantities (manpower, equipment, construction), and operating costs and research. Each major component is composed of many individual elements which are separately assigned monetary values. Considering the thousands of elements which must be identified and also valued, it is evident that this is an extraordinarily complex procedure, feasible only through a vast expenditure of effort on surveillance, data collection, and analysis. So far, only US intelligence agencies have the arsenal of electronic and other resources required for calculations of this detail and scope.

The building-block approach is used by CIA to produce annual estimates of Soviet military expenditures in both ruble values and dollars. The dollar figure is of principal public interest (since it is used for comparison with US expenditures), but it is the CIA ruble estimate which this study uses for its calculation of Soviet military expenditures. Working from the ruble estimate makes it possible to follow the same procedure for conversion to dollars which is used for other countries in this worldwide report and for GNP and other budget expenditures. It also avoids some but not all of the exaggerating effects of the CIA calculation in dollars; these will be discussed below.

In using the CIA ruble estimate for this purpose, however, we do so with reservations. This is not to question either the competence of the analysts, who are highly respected professionals, nor the careful assembly of a massive amount of information. The gaps in knowledge and the need for subjective judgment are still formidable. The numerous uncertainties which invite "worst-case" interpretation and the methodology of the calculations together tend to produce an upward bias in the ruble as well as in the dollar estimate. Even though we cannot remove this bias, or determine precisely how much it may exaggerate the total, identifying some of the factors which appear to produce it may help to indicate the scope of the problem.

Components of CIA estimate

In ruble values, CIA calculates Soviet military expenditures (in 1970 prices) at more than three times the budget of 17.2 billion rubles which the USSR announced for 1979. While the public record does not show how the 1979 figure breaks down into all of the components, averages for the period since 1965 will give some clue to the relative importance of the major categories. The estimate of Soviet expenditures in rubles in that period was composed as follows (ref. 8):

—roughly one-fifth for research, development, test and evaluation (RDT&E);
—one-half for investment (procurement of equipment and construction);
—almost one-third for operating (60 percent of that for personnel).

What does the record say about some of the measurement problems associated with each of these components?

Research—This category of expenditures is identified by the analysts as the most imprecise element in the estimates. Research outlays cannot be estimated from observable physical quantities. Instead they appear to be derived in large part through an analysis of Soviet information on expenditures for science.

While no direct reference to the basis for the calculations seems to have been made recently, analysts indicated in 1974 testimony that a major share of the Soviet science budget was assumed to be military.

CIA stated in 1978 testimony with "high confidence" that the Soviet military RDT&E effort is "large and growing". The estimated increase in this component in the 1970's has been the predominant factor (along with procurement and maintenance of hardware) pushing the overall expenditure total higher (ref. 6). It is the fastest growing of the major components (ref. 8).

An independent study prepared for the National Science Foundation by a specialist in the field reveals some of the practical difficulties in identifying military R&D in Soviet budgets for science (ref. 1). The report provides a careful analysis of definitional and other problems which cannot be adequately summarized here, but two of the general points made seem particularly relevant: a) Soviet reported science budgets appear to be significantly inflated compared with US concepts and b) whether, or how much, Soviet military R&D is included in the science budget is still an unresolved issue.

From this, one could conclude that Soviet budgeting for science is still a largely mysterious area. It may not provide the only basis for the CIA estimate of Soviet expenditures on military R&D, but as a foundation for confident estimates of level or trend it clearly has serious weaknesses.

Investment—The component covering procurement and construction is the part of the estimate in which analysts state they have the greatest confidence. Presumably this is because the numbers of major equipment can, in large part, be observed, and at least some of the ruble prices (e.g., civilian products bought by the military) can be determined from Soviet price lists. Others may be obtained clandestinely. In theory at least there is good, "hard" information in this area. Keeping it accurate and up to date is quite another problem, as evidenced by CIA's announcement in 1976 that Soviet military expenditures in rubles were now estimated to be *twice* as high as previously thought, because the ruble prices paid were higher than CIA had calculated.

Even assuming comparatively solid information in some areas, there are others which must depend heavily on judgment or guesswork, for example: the quality of equipment which is not obtainable or visible by satellite or other observation; the range of efficiency and cost within Soviet industry; and the amount of overhaul of old equipment, a practice which some analysts consider fairly common in the Soviet Union.

In addition, a significant source of measurement error arises in valuing equipment for which no ruble prices are available. The estimating process then becomes very shaky indeed. For many of the procurement items, CIA must use US analogs. Values in US equivalent prices are established, then converted to rubles via a small sample of dollar-ruble ratios (about 1 ruble price for every 10 dollar prices). Assessing quality as compared with like US equipment must become a major headache in this case, made more difficult by the fact that Soviet technology as a rule lags behind the US, and the product itself tends to be more simplified.

For example, CIA testimony mentions microminiaturization in computers as one area in which the Soviets are far behind US technology. The question is how accurately analysts can determine the lesser dollar value of a weapon which does not have built into it the accuracy and capability of remote command and control equivalent to its US counterpart.

Although CIA analysts report that they do make the effort to adjust the cost basis of Soviet equipment for physical and performance qualities, they have stated that where their knowledge is incomplete their estimates tend to overstate the costs of producing the Soviet design.

Operating costs—Manpower, although rated at a lower level of reliability than procurement, is considered by CIA to be the most reliable element in the estimates of Soviet operating costs. It is also a relatively small part of the overall estimate of ruble outlays. While Soviet forces are very large, this is a draft army and ruble pay scales are low. (The pay for a private is said to be the ruble equivalent of about $6 per month not including upkeep).

Estimates of manpower costs presumably depend on the determination of numbers in the total force, the table of organization, and the pay scales used. The record is not clear on all these points. For 1978 CIA estimated manpower at 4.2 million, IISS (the source used in this report) at 3.6 million. The higher CIA figure may result from a definitional difference, possibly from the CIA inclusion of civilians in uniform or of border guards. (ISS has a separate category for paramilitary forces.) It could also result from higher assumptions of the actual complement of Soviet divisions. CIA does state that it takes account of the evidence that a good many Soviet divisions are not at full strength, but certainty in this case may be difficult to establish, and the tendency would be to assume full complement where it is unknown.

1. *Unless specific references are noted, the summary of CIA methodology is drawn from the public record in the annual hearings of the Joint Economic Committee of the US Congress (#5, page 40).*

In addition to the numbers involved, there are unknowns relating to the operational use of Soviet forces for which adjustments may be especially difficult. The Soviet draft provides a work force at the command of the state. For example, recruits are used for agricultural work during the harvest period. The CIA analysts report that they cannot separate out the portion of time the forces are used in essentially civilian work. In other words, Soviet forces are valued as though fully employed in military functions throughout the year.

Whether adequate cost adjustment can be made for relatively low operational use of equipment and lower levels of readiness than in the US is also a question. Officials have at various times referred to these factors, stating that only one-sixth of Soviet navy ships are deployed at sea (US one-third); Soviet strategic subs operate 11 percent; of the time (US 50 percent); pilots with the Soviet air force in Europe fly roughly one-third as much as American pilots; only part of the Soviet ICBM force is kept at peak readiness.

While CIA reports that they do make allowances for these differences, in operating practice, the problems illustrate the inadequacy of number comparisons and complexity of the cost-estimating process even in an area where there is a fair degree of direct knowledge.

Soviet expenditures in dollars

Basis of estimates

The dollar equivalent of the Soviet military effort is now usually determined through one of two basic approaches.

Converting aggregates—Military expenditures in rubles are converted to dollars using the total, or broad categories, of expenditures, with appropriate exchange rates. This is the approach now used in this study. It makes possible the comparison of the military "burden" relative to GNP and other national budgets, and also rough comparisons among countries.

Pricing elements—The alternative method, which is used by CIA, constructs the dollar value of Soviet military expenditures through a building-block approach which parallels that described above for the ruble calculation. In this case every element of the Soviet military force is valued at the price that it would have if purchased in the US. The objective is not to establish the basis for international comparison but to produce a summary indicator of the value of the Soviet military effort in US terms.

Implications of CIA methodology

At first glance the product of the CIA approach seems to meet the requirement for a simple binary match-up: the total of the Soviet military effort, expressed in US costs, appears to have been made comparable with total US military expenditures. In fact, as we have tried to show, the method of calculation is not only based on an extremely fragile structure of evidence but also has built into it an upward bias because of the worst-case assumptions applied to unknowns in the estimating process.

In the CIA dollar calculation, the problems noted above for the ruble estimate are amplified because all components are priced in dollars.

National economies tend to use relatively more of that factor of production in which they have a cost advantage. If, for example, labor is cheap relative to capital, more labor is used. If that labor is valued at prices in effect in an economy where labor costs are high, however, it becomes an extremely expensive item. This is the basis of the distortion which occurs when all elements of the Soviet military effort are given dollar price tags. To offset this distortion, the usual procedure would be to calculate expenditures in the prices of both nations and to take a geometric mean of the dollar and ruble estimates. This is not done in the CIA calculations. For a review of the "index number effect", see ref. 4.

In this limited space it is not possible to summarize the problems and results in detail, or the alternative method of valuing expenditures in dollars. Two examples of the distortions implicit in the dollar valuations are given below.

In arriving at the dollar valuation of Soviet manpower, CIA breaks down the Soviet force into ranks and skill components, applying a dollar-cost factor to each skill level. The average pay for the Soviet force in the dollar calculations comes to about $12,500 per man, according to CIA statements in 1980. The very large Soviet army, bought at low cost in rubles, accounts for about $50 billion when priced at US pay scales. Statements about the 1977 estimates indicated that personnel costs then were 14 percent of total spending in rubles, and 36 percent when calculated in dollars.

The CIA method allows for a difference in composition of US and USSR forces, but it is not at all clear that it adequately covers differences in quality, i.e. the technical qualifications of the force and the equipment available to them. Approximately three-fourths of Soviet manpower are short-term conscripts. Many draftees are unacquainted with the operation of even simple motorized equipment. In contrast, the US has a volunteer, career force, subject to intensive on-the-job training during their years of service. Lower readiness standards in the USSR also reduce training effectiveness, eg. the Soviet air force has relatively less flying time, the army less front-of-the-line equipment for training.

The quality differential is also significant in the dollar pricing of Soviet equipment. In the CIA ruble calculation, some ruble values can be established directly. Dollar valuations, however, are based on US industry's estimates of production costs of samples of Soviet equipment, or on US analogs, which overall are more sophisticated than the Soviet inventory. The adjustments made for quality are subjective judgments and, as recognized by CIA, will have a tendency to overstate Soviet costs.

The agencies preparing the estimates are, of course, aware of the methodological bias inherent in the dollar calculations. In their testimony in 1979, for example, they noted that their "dollar comparisons of US and Soviet defense activities do have a potential bias favoring [i.e., exaggerating] the Soviets, resulting from the index number problem". Despite it, they express a relatively high degree of confidence in the results. In the overall cost estimate, they have usually described the possible margin of error as plus or minus 15 percent. In the 1979 testimony they reduced this to plus or minus 10 percent for the current period.

Professor Holzman's review of the method suggests that because of possible tendencies to worst-case analysis in exercises like this, the range of error in the US-USSR dollar comparisons is likely to be relatively smaller on the low side and much larger on the high side.

WMSE calculations

Soviet Union

The CIA ruble estimate is the basis of the dollar valuation in this publication. For the reasons stated above, it appears to have an upward bias, with the net effect of substantially exaggerating Soviet military expenditures.

The CIA ruble estimate is converted to dollars, in the WMSE method, through exchange rates which the World Bank has been using for calculations of GNP. These rates, tentatively adopted by the Bank in 1979, are the noncommercial (tourist) rates for the ruble and other Eastern European currencies; values established for 1970, the benchmark year,

were moved forward using the US price change in the implicit GNP deflator. At present, the World Bank has this methodology under review, and may make some revisions in it.

The World Bank method assigns a substantially lower value to the ruble than that implicit in the purchasing power estimate of the intelligence calculations, and somewhat lower than the purchasing power estimate previously used in this publication. In adopting an exchange rate conversion in place of purchasing power, we are following the procedure used for other countries.

In view of the uncertain value of the ruble as compared with normally traded currencies, any estimate of its exchange value at this point must be judgmental. Further observation may suggest that it should be assigned a higher value against the dollar — which of course would raise the dollar estimate.

On the other hand, further review of the CIA calculations, by intelligence or other specialists, are quite likely to yield a lower, and we think, a more realistic value of Soviet military expenditures in rubles.

Other Warsaw Pact

WMSE approach—The estimates of military expenditures in the centrally planned economies of Eastern Europe that are members of the Warsaw Pact are based on estimates in national currencies by Dr. Thad Alton and associates (ref. 7). In the Alton estimates, some adjustments are made in the official national figures to conform more closely to US definitions of defense. In converting to dollars, the WMSE method again uses the rates implicit in the World Bank's calculation of GNP.

While there appear to be some differences in factors used, this in general is also the approach adopted by IISS and SIPRI. The total dollar figures for these countries are in fairly close agreement.

Official US approach—The method used in the official US report of military expenditures in the "other WP countries" differs from the above in an important respect: the conversion to dollars calculates military forces separately at equivalent US pay scales. The procedure may be summarized briefly as follows: a) the personnel component of military expenditures is separately estimated in national currencies; b) armed forces (regular and paramilitary) in those countries are then priced in dollars at US pay rates; c) the remainder of the budget is converted to dollars at the purchasing power equivalent rate implicit in the GNP calculations.

The results of this method appear in the ACDA annual report, where they produce military expenditures for the "other WP countries" roughly double the overall estimates of the other sources.

The special personnel adjustment made in the official US estimate of military expenditures for the "other WP countries" affects comparisons between the WP and other countries. There is no indication on the record that this adjustment is made for any other country in the world. If it were done worldwide, it would sharply increase the US Government estimates of military expenditures in other countries. Testimony in 1978 indicates that pricing of other NATO forces at US pay scales would raise the total dollar equivalents of military expenditures for those countries by 22 percent.

* * *

To attempt alternatives to the elaborate official calculations of WP military expenditures is perhaps even more simplistic and risky than to attempt an abbreviated description of the problems. We recognize that the results shown in this publication are not the final answer. Yet somewhere between the upwardly biased official US estimate of $211 billion and the unrealistically low fraction of that which seems to be the official WP version, there must be a reasonable estimate.

At present our approach suggests that military expenditures of the WP countries in 1979 were in total about $83 billion lower than the US Government estimates. Rather than being equal to the NATO expenditures, this would make them lower by 40 percent. A gap like that could make quite a difference in NATO's planning for a continually rising military effort against the competition—and save taxpayers a whale of a lot of money.☐

References—see page 40.

Statistical Sources

The principal sources* are listed first under each topic. Organizations referred to in the text or notes are shown with their initials.

Area and Population United Nations (UN), US Bureau of the Census, Population Reference Bureau, Food and Agriculture Organization of the United Nations (FAO).

Education UNESCO, United Nations (UN), U S Agency for International Development, Organization for Economic Cooperation and Development (OECD), U S Bureau of the Census, World Bank, Population Reference Bureau, U S National Center for Education Statistics, International Monetary Fund.

Exchange Rates International Monetary Fund (IMF), Joint Economic Committee of the U S Congress, World Bank.

Food Food and Agriculture Organization of the United Nations (FAO), U S Department of Agriculture.

Foreign Aid Organization for Economic Cooperation and Development (OECD), U S Central Intelligence Agency (CIA), UN Conference on Trade and Development.

Gross National Product World Bank, Joint Economic Committee of the U S Congress, U S Department of State.

Health World Health Organization (WHO), United Nations (UN), Pan American Health Organization, Organization for Economic Cooperation and Development (OECD), U S Department of Health and Human Services, U S Bureau of the Census, Population Reference Bureau, CREDOC Division d'Economie Medicale, International Social Security Association, International Monetary Fund.

International Peacekeeping United Nations (UN), International Peace Academy, School of Advanced International Studies of Johns Hopkins, United Nations Association of the U S

Labor and Productivity International Labor Organization (ILO), US Bureau of Labor Statistics.

Military International Institute for Strategic Studies (IISS), United Nations (UN), North Atlantic Treaty Organization (NATO), Stockholm International Peace Research Institute (SIPRI), US Agency for International Development, Joint Economic Committee of the US Congress, *The Stateman's Yearbook,* International Labor Organization (ILO), Arms Control and Disarmament Agency (ACDA), US Central Intelligence Agency (CIA), Center for Defense Information, Comptroller General of the US, International Monetary Fund.

Nuclear US Department of Energy, Stockholm International Peace Research Institute (SIPRI), US Department of Defense, US Department of State, *Nuclear News,* US Department of Defense, International Atomic Energy Agency, Union of Concerned Scientists.

Prices World Bank, International Monetary Fund (IMF), U S Department of Commerce.

Refugees U S Committee for Refugees

Research and Development National Science Foundation, Statistical Office of the European Communities, International Energy Agency.

In addition to the sources named, data have been obtained from the regional commissions of the UN and from national statistical services.

References for pages 38-39

1. Campbell, Robert W., *Reference Source on Soviet R&D Statistics 1950-1978,* report prepared for the National Science Foundation, 1978.
2. Central Intelligence Agency, *Estimated Soviet Defense Spending: Trends and Prospects,* June 1978.
3. Central Intelligence Agency, *A Dollar Cost Comparison of Soviet and US Defense Activities, 1967-77,* January 1978.
4. Holzman, Franklyn D., "Are the Soviets Really Outspending the US on Defense?", *International Security,* Spring 1980; also "Is There Really a Military Spending Gap?", House Armed Services Committee, March 16, 1982.
5. Joint Economic Committee, US Congress, *Allocation of Resources in the Soviet Union and China,* 1974-1981 (annual).
6. Joint Economic Committee, US Congress, *Soviet Economy in a Time of Change,* Vol. 1, October 10, 1979, "US and USSR: Comparisons of GNP", by Imogene Edwards, Margaret Hughes, and James Noren.
7. Joint Economic Committee, US Congress, *East European Economic Assessment,* Part 2, July 16, 1981, "East European Defense Expenditures, 1965-78", by Thad P. Alton, Gregor Lazarcik, Elizabeth M. Bass, and Wassyl Znayenko.
8. Select Committee on Intelligence, US Congress, "CIA Estimates of Soviet Defense Spending", Hearings, September 3, 1980.

Doomsday

The Threat of Nuclear War

Like a coiled spring, 50,000 nuclear weapons encircle the globe. Once released, they have the power to end life on earth.

These weapons carry an explosive force equal to 3.5 tons of TNT for every child, woman, and man in the world. They are over one million times more powerful than the Hiroshima bomb.

Is that enough to bring to a halt the manic race for more such weapons? Apparently, not yet. So we must consider the chances and the consequences, for ourselves and our children and the children not yet born, of a coiled spring exploding into its 50,000 incredibly lethal components.

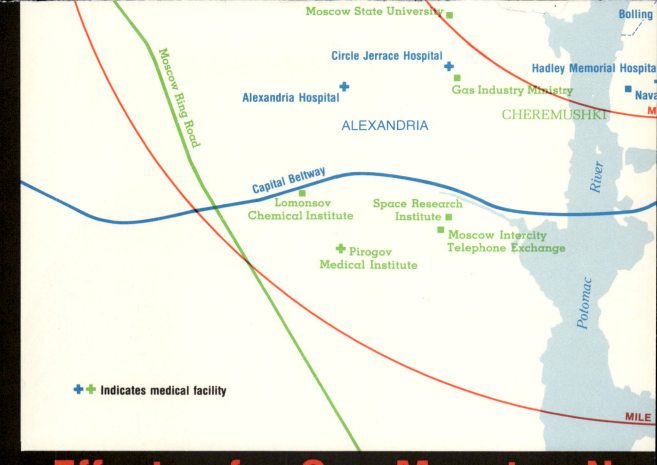

Moscow State University

Bolling

Circle Jerrace Hospital

Hadley Memorial Hospital

Alexandria Hospital

Gas Industry Ministry

Nava

CHEREMUSHKI

Moscow Ring Road

ALEXANDRIA

River

Capital Beltway

Lomonsov
Chemical Institute

Space Research
Institute

Moscow Intercity
Telephone Exchange

Pirogov
Medical Institute

Potomac

✚✚ Indicates medical facility

MILE

Effects of a One-Megaton Nuc

Circles of Death*

Circle 1	**Epicenter**	At ground zero, the surface-burst nuclear weapon (70 times the power of the Hiroshima bomb) creates a crater 300 feet deep and 1,200 feet in diameter. All life and structures are pulverized.
Circle 2	**0-.6 mile**	People, vehicles, buildings, and thousands of tons of earth are swept into a luminous fireball, with temperatures hotter than the sun. The fireball, rising to a height of more than 6 miles and 1 mile wide, incinerates all life below in less than 10 seconds.
Circle 3	**.6-2 miles**	The flash and heat from the explosion sweep outward from the epicenter at the speed of light. A shock wave of compressed air creates overpressures of 100 pounds per square inch at .6 mile to 9 psi at 2 miles. Structures as well as people are crushed. Lethal radiation covers the area. Virtually everyone dies immediately.
Circle 4	**2-3 miles**	Trees, clothes, combustible materials ignite spontaneously. Winds exceed hundreds of miles an hour. Overpressures blow out walls of even the largest buildings. 50 percent of the people die immediately; the rest die more slowly from radioactive poisoning, burns, broken bodies, deeply imbedded fragments of glass.
Circle 5	**3-5 miles**	Frame buildings are blown out or levelled. Fuel storage tanks explode. Intense heat causes third-degree burns to all exposed skin. A firestorm is highly probable; if it occurs, it sucks oxygen out of underground stations, asphyxiating the occupants. Shelters become ovens. 50 percent of the people die immediately; if there is a firestorm, no one survives the day.
Circle 6	**5-10 miles**	The shock wave, travelling 1 mile in 5 seconds, reaches the Capital Beltway and Moscow Ring Road 40 seconds after the blast. People in exposed locations suffer second-degree burns. The scorched area covers 200 square miles. Radioactive fallout creates an immediately lethal zone of 400 square miles, causing death through massive damage to the central nervous system and the bone marrow.

Moving downwind in a huge plume, fallout also contaminates 20,000 square miles, bringing

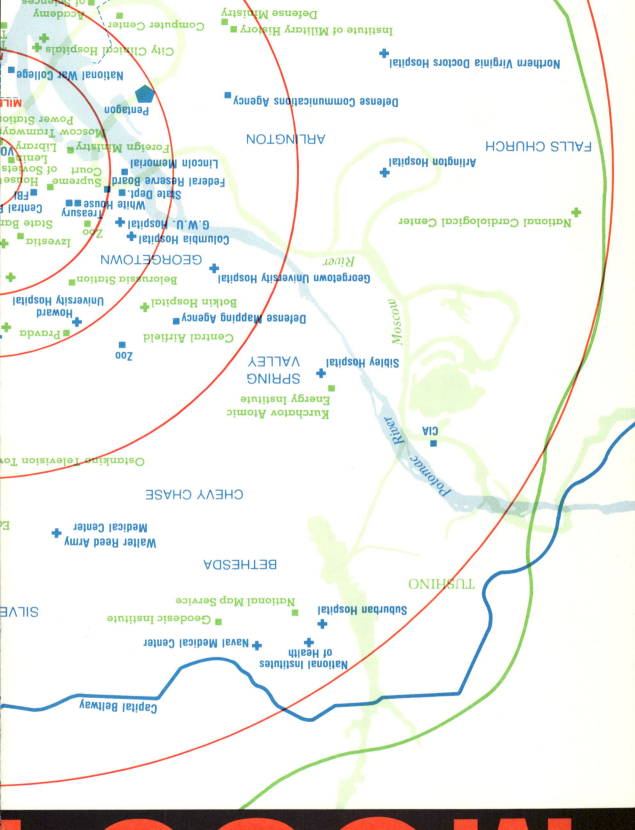

Academy of Sciences

Computer Center

Defense Ministry

Institute of Military History

Northern Virginia Doctors Hospital

City Clinical Hospitals

National War College

Defense Communications Agency

Pentagon

Moscow Tramways
Power Station

ARLINGTON

FALLS CHURCH

Foreign Ministry

Lenin Library

Lincoln Memorial

Supreme Court of Soviets
House

Federal Reserve Board

State Dept.

FBI

White House

Treasury

Central State Bank

Izvestia

Zoo

G.W.U. Hospital

Columbia Hospital

Arlington Hospital

National Cardiological Center

GEORGETOWN

Belorussia Station

Georgetown University Hospital

Moscow River

Howard University Hospital

Botkin Hospital

Pravda

Defense Mapping Agency

Central Airfield

Zoo

Sibley Hospital

SPRING VALLEY

Kurchatov Atomic Energy Institute

Potomac River

CIA

Ostankino Television Tower

CHEVY CHASE

Walter Reed Army Medical Center

BETHESDA

TUSHINO

National Map Service

SILVE

Geodesic Institute

Suburban Hospital

Naval Medical Center

National Institutes of Health

Capital Beltway

MOSC

CHART 14

Nuclear Weapons
The Risk and Consequences

The chances that nuclear weapons will be used are increasing. If used, the probability that general nuclear war will occur is very high indeed. If it does occur, a planetary disaster is assured. This is the coiled spring that threatens doomsday for us all. What could release it?

Risk of Use

The peril of miscalculation, computer malfunction, a deliberate or irrational act that could trigger the use of nuclear weapons, grows with every step forward in nuclear proliferation and weapons modernization.

The sheer size of the stockpiles increases the chance of theft or error. There are thousands of these weapons to be guarded (chart 14). Many are moving, on the high seas, over urban areas and desolate wastes. In transit and in storage they must be protected against terrorist attack, and human or mechanical failure. Major and minor accidents involving nuclear weapons have been frequent enough to be hair-raising. SIPRI has estimated a world average of perhaps one every few months.

The wide dispersion of the weapons and the lengthened lines of communication mean more opportunities for a deliberate or inadvertent break in the chain of control. In time of conventional war, this problem is greatly amplified. Maintaining clear communication lines with submarines and other ships carrying nuclear weapons, and with hundreds of scattered command posts in battle zones would be virtually impossible. In the end, the agonized decision on use may be made by a local commander facing overwhelming odds, and no longer in touch with central authorities.

Technical developments reducing the size and improving the accuracy of nuclear weapons also affect the risk of use. Mini nukes, cruise missiles, mobile deployment, the technical refinements discussed on page 11, are invitations to proliferation and to terrorist attack.

Perhaps most important of all, technical improvements in nuclear weapons have been accompanied by radical change in official concepts of their practical use in war. Visions of first strikes, "surgical strikes," and the graduated use of nuclear weapons in battle are now enshrined in official military policy.

Risk of Escalation

By their very nature these are not war-fighting weapons. They carry immediate death and devastation on a scale unknown in the long history of war. A country or force attacked with them has no defense. Human revulsion against the barbarism of their use could make retaliation inevitable even if other factors did not.

There are, however, other factors in the equation which lead inevitably to escalation. The newest nuclear weapons are now considered to be powerful and accurate enough to hit and destroy the enemy's missiles. This affects the response to an attack, as well as the opponent's original decision to strike. A force under attack, or believing itself to be facing an attack, has a double incentive to respond with its own nuclear weapons. In effect, it must use them or lose them. And using them, the theory goes, may destroy enemy weapons not yet launched, thereby reducing the damage the enemy can inflict.

The speed of delivery puts a premium on computerized systems and automatic response. In the 1950s a bomber would have taken 12 hours to make a 6,000-mile flight. Today an intercontinental missile can deliver its nuclear cargo in under 30 minutes; an offshore submarine in less than 15; a Pershing missile across Europe in 6 minutes. The short flight time means that once an attack is underway, there is simply no time for debate and rational thought. Both warning signals and response are dependent on fragile mechanical systems. These systems have a history of technical failures. There is the fearful possibility that, by accident, they could have triggered the strike in the first place and/or the escalation that follows.

Even with longer warning time military doctrine operates against restraint. The recently-publicized US policy of "decapitation" (which other nuclear states will certainly follow as well) in a sense makes mandatory an automated response to any nuclear attack. The aim of decapitation is to destroy the enemy's political and military command. Knowing this, the authorities have little incentive to withhold response in kind. If successful, the destruction of central authority also eliminates the opportunity to negotiate a halt to the carnage before it is complete. Once the battle is engaged, it becomes an automated fight to the end.

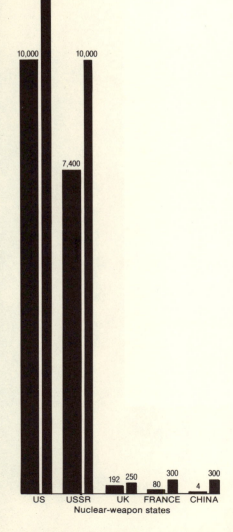

Nuclear Weapons Deployed, 1982

■ Strategic

■ Tactical

20,000

10,000 — 10,000

7,400

10,000

192 250

80

300

4

300

US   USSR   UK   FRANCE   CHINA

Nuclear-weapon states